OSPREY/**AIRWAR** SER

EDITOR: JERRY SCUTT

RAF COMBAT UNITS
SEAC 1941-45

BY BRYAN PHILPOTT

COLOUR PLATES BY
MARTIN HOLBROOK
TOM BRITTAIN
CHRIS WARNER
ARTHUR STURGESS

OSPREY PUBLISHING LONDON

100324407

M62997

940.544942

PHIL

Published in 1979 by
Osprey Publishing Ltd
Member company of the George Philip Group
12–14 Long Acre, London WC2E 9LP
© Copyright 1979 Osprey Publishing Ltd

ISBN 0 85045 297 X

Filmset by BAS Printers Limited, Over Wallop,
Hampshire, England
Printed in Hong Kong

Throughout the campaigns in the Far East, those involved
became used to being called 'The Forgotten Army'. This
appellation was not far from the truth, especially in the dark
days of 1942, and the whole theatre still retains a host of stories
which have not yet been told. In attempting to condense the
broad spectrum of the war in South-East Asia within the few
pages of this book, it was inevitable that oversimplification
would occur, but the author has tried to present a general
picture of the influence of airpower, which was so decisive. In
so doing he has had to highlight certain aspects and
gloss over others. No slight is implied and where individuals or
squadrons have been used as examples these are intended to be
typical of all participants and does not mean that the names of
the unmentioned have been added to 'The Forgotten Army'.

The author is particularly grateful to the following for
information: Wg. Cdr. C. A. C. Stone, DFC, Sqn. Ldr.
'Bush' Cotton, DFC, Sqn. Ldr. L. C. C. Hawkins, Richard
Leask Ward, Geoff Thomas, Mike Bowyer, Chaz Bowyer, and
Bruce Quarrie of Patrick Stephens Ltd.
Unless otherwise stated, all photographs are via R. L. Ward and
the editor acknowledges the additional help of Messrs. C.
Sharman, L. Manwaring and L. Beckford in supplying
photographs to illustrate this volume.

Low pass by Brewster Buffalo WB243 coded RD-B of No. 67 Sqn., believed to have been taken at the time the squadron was based at Mingladon, Rangoon, late in 1941.

The Seeds of War

The reforms introduced by Emperor Meiji which brought Japan from the obscurity of an isolated backwater in which life was simple and followed the pattern of a bygone age had, by the mid-1920s, laid the foundations of ambition. The imitative qualities of the Japanese soon led to the establishment of a life-style closely aligned to that of the Western powers. The acceptance of railways, electric power, telephones, modern transportation, parliamentary elections, a sound educational system, and the formation of a modern army and navy, all contributed to the desire to further emulate the Western powers by the accumulation of an empire. What the French and British had done in the eighteenth and nineteenth centuries became the twentieth-century goal of the Japanese. The acquisition of Korea, Formosa, and the Pescadores Islands, as well as a decisive influence in Manchuria, did not go unnoticed, with the result that in 1918 Britain and the United States took steps to apply a brake on Japan's expansionist policies.

In the early 1920s, the rulers of Japan were liberal-minded and agreed to the Anglo-American plans, which limited military expansion by placing restrictions on the production of weapons, as well as a proportional equipping programme in which the ratio of tactical and strategic weapons was directly related to those of Britain and America. It was during this time that the British

government sent an air mission to Japan to train the Imperial Japanese Naval Air Service to the standards befitting a major air power. The mission took with it a variety of British training and combat aircraft, including six Sopwith Cuckoo torpedo-bombers, machines which allowed the current British enthusiasm for torpedo bombing to be fully exploited. The mission found its pupils to be enthusiastic about this method of attack, and the pilots concerned to be well above average. Thus in 1921 was the die cast, and from these small but seemingly insignificant beginnings the IJNAS gradually perfected the basics it had been taught, which two decades later were to be demonstrated with frightening efficiency in the Pacific.

Although it would appear that not a great deal of interest was taken in the development of Japanese airpower, after the return of the mission the possibility of war with Japan was at least acknowledged by the Americans, who, in 1924, formulated plans for suitable counter-measures.

Being an island nation, Japan, like Britain, relied on raw materials from overseas sources; her relative poverty in mineral resources, especially oil, meant that she had to set about obtaining her own markets if she was to become a major world power. During the 1930s Japan had been invading China in search of part of the wealth she coveted.

3

Sqn. Ldr. C. A. C. Stone in the cockpit of Hurricane BE171 at Mingladon in February 1942. The rank pennant was added after the action of 27 January 1942. (C. A. C. Stone)

The remains of F/Off. Strut's No. 135 Sqn. Hurricane after it had been bounced by enemy fighters while landing at Rangoon. Strut, a New Zealander, was only slightly injured in the crash. (L. Hawkins)

In 1931 Manchuria was annexed, and the Japanese military machine was poised to look for further conquests on the Chinese mainland.

Reports from the war in China indicated that the Japanese had acquired some modern and effective equipment, especially in the form of fighters and bombers. Reports of these aircraft were filtered back to the Western powers, but it was assumed that they were grossly exaggerated and that most of Japan's airpower consisted of inferior copies of British and American designs.

The wealth Japan needed to become strong and self-sufficient belonged to European colonial powers; French Indo-China was rich in rice, the Federated Malay States and Burma, which belonged to Britain, had tin, oil and rubber, whilst the Netherlands East Indies also had a plentiful supply of oil. The outbreak of war in Europe in 1939, followed by the German victories in 1940, considerably reduced the ability of the Western powers to defend their possessions in the Far East. In 1940 Japan signed a defence pact with Germany and Italy, and in 1941, under an agreement with the French, moved troops into the southern area of Indo-China. In China the war was going badly for Chiang Kai-Shek, and in December 1940, in an attempt to aid her Chinese ally, the United States imposed a ban on the sale of raw materials to Japan.

Throughout the summer of 1941 the Japanese sought to achieve their ambitions by political negotiations with a view to being allowed a free hand to expand southwards to the East Indies. In this America saw a threat to her own influence throughout the Pacific, and resisted all such requests. The embargo placed on Japan was gradually strangling her ambitions, and despite stringent rationing of fuel oil, it became apparent that unless steps were taken to provide this essential ingredient her armed forces would grind to a standstill.

By surrendering her interests in China, Japan could

Curtiss Mohawk BT471 of No. 155 Sqn. The A1 Type fuselage roundels and equal division fin flash date the picture prior to June 1942 and it was possibly taken during the squadron's formation at Peshawar in April 1942.

have eased the embargo, but she was reluctant to do this. Therefore, the alternative of seizing the mineral-rich areas needed became more a necessity than a choice. The invasion of Russia by Hitler eased the threat of an attack by her natural enemy on Japan's northern flank, so by the autumn of 1941 the time seemed right for positive action to be taken.

Taking stock of the oil situation in November 1941 showed that unless Japan withdrew from China and denounced her pact with Germany and Italy, thus removing trading restrictions, her supplies would be exhausted by the end of 1943. The situation therefore was one whereby the Japanese would have to fight for their needs, since political alternatives were unacceptable—and the time to strike was whilst stocks were at a high level. The philosophy behind this thinking came from those responsible for the expansion of the war in China and appears to have paid no more than lip service to the vast industrial potential of the United States. On the other hand, the Japanese government believed that it could not win a long struggle against the USA, but they were influenced by the navy chiefs, who claimed that victory could be theirs if the struggle lasted no more than two years.

During the months of political wrangling, military strategists worked on producing a plan that was acceptable to both the army and navy. The most obvious course of action was a direct attack on the Indies, followed by the invasion of the Philippines and Malaya, which would, however, have left the flanks open for counter-attacks from the British and Americans. The navy favoured a step-by-step campaign through the Indies to Malaya, but the army opposed this on the basis that such a steady advance

allowed too much time for defences to be strengthened. Army thinking favoured an attack overland through Malaya to the Indies, bypassing the Philippines altogether. In the end a compromise was reached whereby a simultaneous advance along both lines of attack would be made through Malaya and the Philippines to the Indies. This was an ambitious plan which would need the utmost co-operation and co-ordination in timing, but if all aspects went as planned it would overwhelm the limited defences the Japanese knew would oppose them.

As far as land-based forces were concerned, those available to the Allies were numerically superior to the Japanese, but they were widely dispersed over thousands of square miles; at sea the Japanese fleet was more than equal to any force that could be quickly mustered by the defenders and included a large number of carriers with a sizeable air element, which could strike at land bases that were immune from attack by land-based aircraft. In fact the whole Pacific sea war was to be dominated by carrier-based aircraft, aircraft carriers becoming the 'new' capital ships of the fleets involved—a fact quickly realized by the Allies.

The events of 7 December 1941, when aircraft from six Japanese aircraft carriers struck at the American fleet in Pearl Harbor, have been well documented and are outside the scope of this narrative. It should, however, be recorded that as a result of this attack Hitler decided to declare war

5

Sqn. Ldr. Stone flanked by two pilots of No. 135 Sqn. in front of a Hurricane IIc at Yelahanka. (C. A. C. Stone)

on America, and thus helped seal his own fate. He had no reason to take this action, for although the Americans were to a certain extent committed to help in Europe with the supply of arms, not all their politicians were convinced that total involvement there was necessary, indeed many of them deprecated a war on two fronts.

Hitler could offer nothing to the Japanese, who did not in any case need his help, and the sole result of his action was to bring together the military and industrial power of America and Russia against Germany in total world war, with an inevitable outcome the longer it progressed.

On the same day that Pearl Harbor was attacked, but on the other side of the International Date Line, where it was 8 December, Japanese troops landed on the north-east coast of Malaya, and the fortress of Singapore was attacked from the air; the British defences in the area were about to be most severely tested.

Singapore

Separating the Indian Ocean from the South China Sea, the Malay Peninsula forms a natural barrier to sea-going traffic plying between Europe and the Orient. Access to eastern ports must therefore be gained by following the Strait of Malacca, between the southern tip of Malaya and the island of Sumatra. The island of Singapore, located at the tip of the peninsula and separated from the mainland by the Johore Strait, was therefore of considerable strategic value to the British, who chose it as the location for a naval base when they started to strengthen the Singapore defences in 1921.

It was the growth of Japanese power that led to the British decision to take a close look at the defence of the Malay Peninsula, and their first thoughts were the creation of a powerful Far East fleet. Cut-backs in defence expenditure in the 1920s prevented the creation of such a fleet, so the alternative was to build a base from which the main British fleet could operate, the idea being that elements of this fleet could steam to Singapore from European waters in time of crisis. During this period of minimum expenditure on defence, the thought of airpower taking a dominant part in any future war was almost inconceivable; an attack of this nature on Singapore was believed to be impossible, and as approach to the island through the northern end of the Malay Peninsula was considered to be out of the question due to the dense jungle, inhospitable landscape and climate: any future threat must, it was felt, come from seawards.

With these thoughts in mind Singapore Island was gradually turned into what was thought to be an impregnable fortress. By the time the war in Europe started in September 1939, the island fortress was ready; more troops were assigned to Malaya than had ever been garrisoned there before, and batteries of guns, including five 15-inch weapons, of the type fitted to most capital ships, bristled on the seaward side. Aircraft, however, were very few in number and reinforcement squadrons were only half of what had been promised, but Singapore was considered secure; even with the lack of a Far East fleet it was considered that the defenders could hold out for the time, estimated at seventy days, it would take for fleet reinforcements to arrive from Europe or the Indian Ocean.

An effective air raid warning system was non-existent, and it was not until the reinforcement period for the arrival of the fleet was extended to 180 days that doubts began to occur. This new period of time meant that the garrison would need to hold the island for six months before support could be given, during which time it was quite possible that the Japanese would develop airfields in Thailand as well as northern Malaya from which they could mount air strikes. The air commander in Malaya, Air Marshal John Babington, proposed that the only solution was to rely on airpower for defence, and his proposal was supported by Sir Shenton Thomas, the Governor of the Straits Settlements. But at this time London could not see that Japan would be the aggressor, and even when the new army commander, Major-General Lionel Bond, reaffirmed in mid-1940 that Malaya must be held and he could only do this if sufficient airpower was available, a review of the situation was not made until August. At this time the RAF had only eighty-eight aircraft on the peninsula, most of which were obsolete when compared with those in use in Europe. Agreement was reached that this force would have to be expanded to at least 366 first-line aircraft and the army garrison doubled. These recommendations were approved by the Cabinet, but there was still disagreement between the Prime Minister, Winston Churchill, and the Chiefs of Staff. The former, in Vol. II of *The Second World War*, is quoted as saying at this time that he did not consider Japan to be on

A No. 135 Sqn. Hurricane under repair at Yelahanka. The size of the wing roundel and proportions of the fin flash are of interest, as are the exposed structural details. (C. A. C. Stone)

The man with the camera diverting the attention of local Burmese from a No. 357 Sqn. Lysander, which has a long-range tank fitted and wheel spat panels removed.

the verge of war, and even if she were it was unlikely that she would undertake so major a venture as an attack on Singapore, but if she did the prime defence of Singapore was the fleet and that defence must therefore be based on a strong local garrison and the general potentials of seapower. Despite this assumption the army, navy and air force commanders increased their demands for a minimum air strength of 566 aircraft.

Air Marshal Sir Robert Brooke-Popham became Commander-in-Chief Far East in late 1940, and midway through the following year Air Vice-Marshal Conway Pulford replaced Babington as the Far East air commander. By late autumn 1941, instead of the 566 aircraft proposed by his predecessors and the 366 approved in London, Pulford had a total of 158 divided among nine RAF squadrons, five Australian and two New Zealand. Fighter defence was in the hands of American-built Brewster Buffalo aircraft, which Brooke-Popham had assured everyone were superior to Japanese fighters, and obsolete Bristol Blenheim night-fighters, which equipped one squadron, No. 27.

Two strike squadrons, Nos. 36 and 100, were equipped with the ancient Vickers Vildebeeste with which to carry out torpedo attacks against enemy shipping, and No. 205 Sqn. had Catalina flying-boats for use in the reconnaissance role. Blenheims and Australian-crewed Hudsons provided the main bomber and photographic reconnaissance aircraft. The grand total of Pulford's air force when war came on 8 December was 362 aircraft, of which 233 were serviceable. Of the 52 Buffaloes in reserve, 21 were also unserviceable due to trouble with engine valve gear, a fault which led to No. 67 Sqn., then in Burma, to ground all its aircraft during the first week of December.

In late October the battleship *Prince of Wales* had been ordered to join forces with the battle cruiser *Repulse*, and, together with four destroyers and the aircraft carrier *Indomitable*, sailed for Singapore. Unfortunately *Indomitable* ran aground off Jamaica, so when the other vessels arrived in Singapore on 2 December, they had no air cover. This duty was assigned to the Buffaloes of No. 453 Sqn. RAAF, based at Sembawang.

Increasing Japanese activity in November indicated that some move was afoot, but there was still a marked reluctance on the part of the British to accept that Malaya might be in any danger. Churchill still doubted the power of the Japanese forces, and Brooke-Popham considered that the Soviet Union was a more likely target. Others underestimated the fighting qualities of Japanese troops and there was a widely held belief that their airpower consisted of short-sighted, ill-trained aircrew flying inferior machines.

The first positive indication that an attack on Malaya was imminent came on 6 December when a Hudson of No. 1 Sqn. RAAF, flown by Flt. Lt. J. C. Ramshaw, spotted a convoy of Japanese ship some 300 miles off the coast. Another Hudson made similar sightings, but analysis of these reports and interrogation of the pilots failed to indicate whether or not they had seen two separate convoys, the same one, or where the ships were heading.

Flt. Lt. L. Hawkins pictured with a Hurricane destined for No. 135 Sqn. during a stop on a Far East ferry flight. The machine shows a C1 fuselage roundel with a Type B on the wing and long-range tanks in place; the legend on the panel by the pilot's leg reads, ACC Fitted. Do not remove.' (L. Hawkins)

Flight-Lieutenant Ramshaw did in fact request permission to shadow the ships he had sighted, but this request was refused. Early on the morning of 7 December two Catalina flying-boats of No. 205 Sqn. took off to carry out further reconnaissance and both failed to return. It is believed that the second of these was shot down by Japanese fighters operating from a newly constructed airfield on Phu Quoc Island. If this is so, it was the first act of war in the Pacific and the RAF's first loss due to enemy action.

Throughout 7 December Air Vice-Marshal Pulford kept as many reconnaissance aircraft as possible in the air in an attempt to locate the previously sighted Japanese fleet and discover its intentions. But storms and thick cloud prevented any positive location and it was not until the early evening that what was thought to be a cruiser and four other ships were sighted. In the meantime Sir Robert Brooke-Popham was in something of a dilemma as to whether or not he should authorize the go-ahead for Operation 'Matador'. This was the code name for a British plan to occupy parts of Thailand in the event of signs of a Japanese move. It was feared that such an act might be considered as aggression by the Thais if made too early, and Brooke-Popham was continually given varying degrees of authority. On 5 December he had been told to act on his own initiative if Singora or Patani came under threat, but at this time there was no positive proof that this would be the case. Bearing in mind that British policy was to avoid war with Japan, Brooke-Popham's hesitancy can be understood; similarly any attack on the reported Japanese fleet would also mark the British as the aggressors.

While discussions were held and signals flashed beween Singapore and London, the Japanese force moved relentlessly on. Just before midnight on 7 December ships were reported anchoring off the beaches north-east of Kota Bharu, and just after midnight troops started to come ashore. There could no longer be any doubts that Malaya was under attack, and Air Vice-Marshal Pulford ordered his air force into action, the first objective being to bomb the enemy forces landing at Kota Bharu.

Blenheims of Nos. 27 and 62 squadrons as well as Hudsons of the RAAF and two Buffaloes of No. 243 Sqn. bombed and strafed the beaches with some success, sinking landing barges as well as causing casualties among the troops. Some of the No. 27 Sqn. Blenheims failed to find their objective owing to bad weather and returned to Sungei Patani to refuel. The same storms also prevented No. 62 Sqn. from carrying out the planned attack, but it flew on to Patani and bombed Japanese transport barges.

The main Japanese invasion forces came ashore at Singora and Patani, where the Thai Army formally surrendered, thus giving the invaders complete access to the airfields at these locations, a situation that was originally planned to be prevented by 'Matador'. Instead of immediately attacking these enemy-occupied airfields in strength, the bomber force available to Pulford continued to attack the beaches at Kota Bharu, giving the Japanese time to assemble some air strength with which to strike at the RAF airfields in northern Malaya.

In the meantime Singapore suffered its first air raid at approximately 0430hrs, when nine Mitsubishi G3M *Nell*

A pleasing view of a No. 28 Sqn. Hurricane IIb, HL857, fitted with long-range fuel tanks.

Spitfires, Mosquitoes, Thunderbolts and Sea Otters are visible in this view of an unrecorded location. The nearest Otter is JN193, a Mk I, and all three are believed to have been on the strength of a SEAC communications/rescue unit.

bombers roared overhead. The lights of the city blazed out to give the Japanese crews easy target identification, but no Allied aircraft were scrambled and the raiders were met by anti-aircraft fire and searchlights. The main targets were the airfields at Tengah and Seletar, but little damage was done to these two bases; a few bombs fell in the city centre, where buildings were destroyed and approximately 180 casualties, sixty of which were fatal, occurred.

Just before 0700hrs a series of attacks on Allied airfields commenced at Sungei Patani, when five Mitsubishi Ki-21 *Sally* bombers, operating from the occupied bases in Thailand, swept in from the west, catching the Buffaloes of No. 21 Sqn. and the Blenheims of No. 27 Sqn. on the ground. The Australian squadron was refused permission to scramble the Buffaloes; two aircraft had already taken off without having waited for orders, but the warning had not come early enough and the Buffaloes could not gain enough height to intercept the bombers. Even if they had, it would have been a fruitless exercise since neither aircraft's guns would operate due to faulty solenoids; a problem which often beset the unfortunate Buffalo. By the time the Japanese force withdrew, No. 27 Sqn. had lost eight of its twelve Blenheims and the Australian Buffalo squadron had two of its aircraft destroyed and five damaged.

Some three hours later fifteen *Nell*s returned to carry on the devastation, but again the Buffaloes were not scrambled. By mid-afternoon Sungei Patani was declared unusable and the remnants of No. 27 Sqn. and their Australian colleagues moved to Butterworth, which had also been attacked throughout the day.

During this series of raids No. 62 Sqn. at Alor Star had also been caught on the ground and lost all but two of its Blenheims, but working through the night, ground crews managed to repair some aircraft which the following day were also moved to Butterworth. Raids had concentrated on the airfields mentioned as well as those at Penang and Butterworth, the Japanese using fragmentation bombs with the aim of causing damage to aircraft and personnel but leaving the airfields fit for their occupation during the advance down the peninsula. By the evening of 8 December only fifty of the original 110 RAF aircraft in northern Malaya were in an airworthy condition; those that remained were to be used the following day to strike back at the enemy.

When positive confirmation of Japanese occupation of the airfields at Singora and Patani was received, Nos. 34 and 62 Sqns. were detailed to attack these objectives. Six Blenheims from No. 34 Sqn. left Butterworth to attack Singora, and although they reached their objective, despite the lack of the promised Buffalo fighter escort, they lost three of their number in the ensuing fight over the Japanese base. Late in the afternoon the three remaining Blenheims of No. 34 Sqn., plus the patched aircraft of No. 62 Sqn., were bombed-up at Butterworth for a return raid on Singora.

First aircraft airborne was Blenheim L1134/PT-F piloted by acting Sqn. Ldr. A. K. S. Scarf. As he gained height a force of Japanese bombers arrived and bombed the airfield and taxying Blenheims. Scarf was helpless to intervene and could only keep out of the way, hoping that some of his colleagues could join him. His hopes were in vain; all the remaining Blenheims were destroyed and Scarf would have been quite justified in abandoning his mission. But the destruction of his squadron only increased his determination to hit back at the enemy, so he swung his aircraft onto course for Singora. Scarf, who had joined the RAF in 1936, was a highly skilled pilot, never happier than when demonstrating his prowess at manoeuvring his Blenheim to its limits. He needed all the skill he could muster as he flew the aircraft at low level towards his target.

Japanese fighters made several half-hearted attempts to intercept the Blenheim, but Scarf's gunner, Flt. Sgt. C. Rich, kept them at bay with his Lewis gun. The apparent lack of determination by the Japanese pilots was probably due to dwindling fuel, but no such problem faced those who intercepted the lone bomber when it reached Singora and started its bombing run. Making a steady run across the airfield Scarf released his bombs, whilst Rich in the turret sprayed the rows of parked aircraft with deadly effect. The gunner's attention soon had to move to more mobile aircraft, as twelve fighters descended for the kill. Scarf threw the Blenheim from side to side at tree-top height in his efforts to present a difficult target to his adversaries, and Rich kept up an accurate counter-attack which consumed seventeen drums of ammunition. But the odds were stacked too high and the Blenheim was riddled from nose to tail. Scarf was wounded several times, and collapsed across the controls on one occasion. He was pulled away from them by Flt. Sgt. Calder and Rich, who evacuated his turret to help.

Rich continued to support the mortally wounded pilot as the Blenheim headed south, the crew's problems being somewhat eased when they crossed the Thai border and the Japanese fighters withdrew. Scarf decided to land at Alor Star and put the aircraft down in fields adjacent to the hospital, which may have been a deliberate action, the pilot having elected to ignore the runway in an attempt to receive quicker medical attention, but this is not by any means certain. The other two crew members lifted Scarf from the cockpit and laid him on the Blenheim's wing, where a doctor administered morphia before having him removed to the hospital. A blood transfusion was carried out, two pints incidentally coming from Scarf's wife Elizabeth, who was a nurse at the hospital, but he died soon after admission to the operating theatre. In 1946, when the story of his valour was made known to the authorities, Arthur Scarf was awarded a much-deserved posthumous Victoria Cross.

The severe punishment received by Pulford's air force dramatically underlined the powerful effect of superior

Hurricane IIc BP 704 of No. 28 Sqn. over the Chindwin River in 1943. The dimensions of the national insignia make interesting comparison with the previous picture of a partially stripped No. 135 Sqn. machine.

Sqn. Ldr. Stone briefs pilots of No. 17 Sqn. prior to an attack on Japanese troops advancing through Burma. (C. A. C. Stone)

Late in the afternoon of 8 December the two warships set sail and soon afterwards a signal was flashed to them confirming that the air cover requested was not possible. Phillips accepted this quite philosophically and told his commanders that they would just have to proceed without it. The Japanese had intended to attack the *Prince of Wales* and *Repulse* whilst they were anchored in Singapore harbour, and a reconnaissance flight on 9 December reported that they were still there. At about the same time as this report was received the Japanese submarine I-65 also reported seeing the battle fleet at sea. Clearly both reports could not be correct, and when the aircraft's photographs were developed they proved to be of two cargo ships, so the submarine commander's report had been correct. The fate of the British fleet was virtually sealed. Japanese aircraft that had been bombed-up ready to attack the ships in Singapore were hastily rearmed and on the morning of 10 December a force comprising fifty-two torpedo-bombers and thirty-three conventionally armed bombers took off from their base.

Action stations sounded aboard the British ships at 1107hrs and the anti-aircraft guns opened fire at 1115hrs, engaging *Nell* bombers. In spite of accurate fire the *Nell*s maintained their formation and bombed, hitting the *Repulse* amidships but not causing any great damage. But soon after the torpedo-bombers arrived, and the lack of British fighters enabled them to make almost leisurely attacks, which commenced at 1140hrs. The *Prince of Wales* was crippled by several hits. The *Repulse* was soon also under attack, and despite superb seamanship by her captain she was hit many times. The air/sea action continued at a tremendous pace, with the Japanese squadrons giving no respite to the two ships. At 1230hrs the *Repulse* was abandoned by her crew and forty minutes later the *Prince of Wales*' resistance also ended when her crew took to the boats. About the time the waves closed over the *Prince of Wales* Buffaloes of No. 453 Squadron RAAF, which had been scrambled from Singapore, arrived over the scene, too late to provide anything more than cover for the rescuers. In just over two hours, at a cost of four aircraft destroyed and fourteen damaged, the Japanese had wiped out the heart of the British Far East Fleet, as well as dealing another severe blow to morale, which was already falling very quickly as a result of the reverses on land and in the air.

On the same day that the two British capital ships were sunk, all aircraft that were still capable of flying were ordered to retreat south to the airfield at Ipoh. Only two Blenheims of No. 27 Sqn. made the journey to the new base and the Australian Buffalo squadrons also suffered very badly. By Christmas it was obvious that Singapore Island was the only refuge available, and this could not hold out unless more modern fighter aircraft were made available. Throughout the period of retreat down the Malay Peninsula the only RAF Buffalo-equipped squadron, No. 243, had been based at Kallang on Singapore Island.

airpower, and no one was in any doubt now about the quality of the Japanese aircraft or their pilots. The wreckage of Allied aircraft and devastated airfields provided positive evidence that Japanese airpower was not the myth many believed it to be, and within three days of the invasion at Kota Bharu another costly lesson was to lay another myth dear to the Royal Navy.

Admiral Tom Phillips's Eastern Fleet could not stand by whilst the land and air battles continued, so he decided to put to sea in an attempt to engage the Japanese naval force that had supported the landings at Singora and Patani. The lack of a carrier was a handicap and, with the northern airfields denied him, Pulford could not guarantee air cover. But Phillips had no doubts of the ability of the battle cruisers *Prince of Wales* and *Repulse* and their destroyer support group to outgun and outrun anything the Japanese task force had. His main concern was submarines, but he felt that by steering east of the Anamba Islands he could avoid most of the submarines and outsteam the rest. Any concern about attack by bombers or torpedo-aircraft was secondary, for Phillips was a firm believer in the ability of warships to withstand air attacks, especially if their anti-aircraft weapons were plentiful and well manned. Air reconnaissance ahead of the fleet looked to be possible, but the situation was still very fluid and losses of aircraft caught on the ground was still seriously depleting the force available to the air commander.

Sharing the defence of the island with the RAF Buffaloes were the remnants of the two Australian squadrons, now combined to form one unit, No. 488 Sqn., and a squadron of the Royal Netherlands Indies Army Air Corps, which had moved in from Java. In attempts to make the Buffaloes more effective, components were removed to improve streamlining, and the two wing-mounted .50in guns were replaced by .303in weapons. These actions, together with reduced fuel and ammunition loads, certainly helped, but the rotund Brewster fighter was still no match for the aircraft of the Japanese fighter squadrons. The Buffaloes fought valiantly and did succeed in providing useful support for the army by strafing ground troops and convoys. But in air-to-air combat they suffered very badly. No. 243 Sqn. claimed the first Japanese raider to be destroyed over Singapore on 10 January 1942, but by the end of the month nearly all its aircraft had been lost in raids on Kallang.

Much-needed reinforcements in the form of Hurricanes arrived on 13 January, and these were assembled and ready for action a week later when pilots of Nos. 17, 135 and 136 Sqns., together with ground crews, were formed into No. 232 Sqn. Their success was immediate as eight from a formation of 27 Japanese bombers fell to the guns of the Hurricanes on 20 January. But success was short-lived, for the following day the bombers appeared with an escort of Mitsubishi A6M2 fighters, which shot down five of the Hurricanes. The British fighters had been diverted from the Middle East and were fitted with tropical filters, which reduced their top speed by about 30mph, and they were no match for the *Zero* when combat was fought on level terms.

More Japanese landings took place at Endau on 25 January and eight Hurricanes together with fifteen Buffaloes escorted Hudsons, Blenheims and Vildebeestes detailed to bomb troops and landing craft. Twelve *Zeros* were shot down, but in view of the aircraft available to the

Sterling work was done by the Vultee Vengeance in the Far East, the only theatre where the RAF used dive bombers to any extent. Here a trio of aircraft of No. 84 Sqn. pass over the Chindwin in 1944.

The first Spitfires in the Far East were PR Vs, which were sent to No. 681 Sqn. at Dum Dum, Calcutta. This machine, serialled in the BR range, created great interest amongst American personnel there, as it was the first example of the type they had seen. (C. Sharman)

Lysander T1688 of No. 357 Sqn. at Drigh Road, July 1945.

Japanese such a rate of attrition could easily be withstood. By the end of January only eight Hurricanes of No. 232 Sqn. remained at Kallang, further replacements having been diverted to Sumatra in view of the deteriorating situation in Malaya. Hurricanes from No. 258 Sqn. and those remaining with No. 232 Sqn. continued to fly sorties over Singapore until the garrison finally surrendered on 15 February.

During the fighting in Malaya a total of 390 RAF aircraft had been destroyed for the loss of 92 Japanese; in the hectic battles over Singapore, Hurricanes achieved over 100 victories but lost 45 of their number. It was very much a case of far too little, far too late. If Hurricanes had been available in greater quantities from the very beginning of the Japanese invasion things may have turned out a little differently.

After the surrender of Singapore, Hudsons and Blenheims withdrew to Sumatra, where they formed No. 225 (Bomber) Group, and mounted attacks on convoys and the Malayan mainland. For a short while the remaining bombers, escorted by Hurricanes, achieved some success, including the annihilation of a Japanese task force dispatched to occupy Sumatra. But the odds were overwhelming, despite a gallant rearguard action by the Hurricanes of Nos. 232 and 605 Sqns., which fought side by side with Dutch Kittyhawks and Buffaloes, the end was inevitable and on 8 March the Dutch army commander surrendered.

With Hong Kong surrendering on Christmas Day, Borneo falling the next day, Singapore in February and Sumatra in early March, the Japanese had, in less than 100 days, taken a giant step towards obtaining the empire they coveted.

Burma

Forming a natural barrier between Malaya and India, Burma, with its mountain ranges, three rivers, steep valleys, and a climate which could bring drought conditions on the one hand or monsoons with up to 500 inches of rain on the other, presented one of the most inhospitable countries to defend or attack. The conquest of Burma would open the vast riches of India to the Japanese as well as isolate their old enemy, China, from her main source of supply. Whereas the British had considered the jungle to be an area in which fighting was impossible, the Japanese had other ideas. Their advance through the Malayan jungle to the backdoor of Singapore proved that such terrain was neutral and could be overcome if proper methods were used. Similar tactics would also work for them in Burma, so the Allied troops assigned to defend this dense green foliage, in which natural pests and hazards gave more than enough problems to cope with, also found themselves facing a cunning and determined enemy, experienced in the art of jungle warfare.

In December 1941 the air defence of Burma was in the hands of No. 67 Sqn. RAF equipped with Buffaloes and the legendary American Volunteer Group, or to give them their more romantic name, the Flying Tigers. Led by Claire Chennault, the AVG flew Curtiss P-40s, its main objective being the defence of the Burma Road—the only land link between India and Burma. But Chiang Kai-Shek had allowed the AVG to move south in search of action over Rangoon, which, being Burma's only port, was a major target for the Japanese, who had over 400 aircraft with which to spearhead their attack.

Rangoon suffered its first air raid on Christmas Eve, by which time RAF reinforcements were on their way. One of the squadrons posted to Burma was No. 17, which had left the Clyde in the troopship *Durban Castle* on 9 December 1941. The original planned destination of the squadron was the Middle East, but Pearl Harbor was attacked during the sea passage and it was diverted to the Far East. Some of the pilots and ground crews were transferred to Pan American flying-boats, which made their way to Burma via India. 'A' Flight of No. 17 Sqn. went to Singapore to fly its Hurricanes in the defence of the island, whilst 'B' Flight, with the squadron CO, Sqn. Ldr. C. A. C. Stone, and Sqn. Ldr. Frank Carey, the CO of No. 135 Sqn., arrived at Mingladon. Carey went on to Zayatkwin thirty miles north-east of Rangoon to await the arrival of his aircraft.

When the cadre of No. 17 Sqn. arrived at Mingladon it found that the sixteen Buffaloes of No. 67 Sqn., together with the P-40s of the AVG, had been putting up spirited resistance against the mounting Japanese attacks. The Buffaloes were no match for the enemy fighters, but against Mitsubishi Ki-21-1a bombers they had enjoyed some success, claiming at least thirty-seven in the raids on Rangoon, which had caused over 7,000 casualties. But attrition was taking its toll and by early January only four Buffaloes remained airworthy. On the 23rd of the month No. 17's frustration in being merely spectators looked to be coming to an end, when the first three Hurricanes arrived

from the Middle East. These were Mk IIb aircraft, armed with twelve .303 Browning machine-guns, four of which were immediately removed by No. 17 Sqn. to give the aircraft greater manoeuvrability. The three aircraft were still in Middle East camouflage and were also fitted with tropical filters, which cut down their top speed. They were also fitted with long-range wing tanks, which were to cause considerable embarrassment to Sqn. Ldr. Stone in more ways than one.

Almost as soon as the new aircraft had landed and been refuelled, the air raid warning went. Squadron Leader Stone, together with Flt. Lt. Penny-Leigh and F/Off. J. Elsdon, scrambled. Hampered by the tanks the three Hurricanes took nearly twenty minutes to reach 10,000ft, from which height Stone saw what he took to be a dog fight going on between the AVG and raiding Ki-21-1a bombers. Whilst getting his flight into position to dive in support of the P-40s, Stone's three Hurricanes were 'bounced' by ten Nakajima Ki-27a *Nate* fighters. Stone and his companions had heard stories of myopic Japanese pilots who couldn't shoot straight, flying outdated aircraft, but in the next few

Equally legendary, albeit in a less spectacular way, were the exploits of the SEAC Dakota squadrons, which became the life-line of the ground troops slogging through the Burmese jungle. Aircraft 'S' of an unknown unit shows typical SEAC markings of the latter war period, with the serial presented under the fin flash and squadron letters on the nose.

Playing a unique combat role in RAF hands in SEAC was the Republic Thunderbolt, over 800 of which were delivered in two main marks—I (P-47D razorback) and II (P-47D-25 and subsequent models with bubble hood). Pictured at Ratnap in late 1944 was HD244/HT-Z of No. 258 Sqn. in green/earth camouflage and SEAC identity bands common to the type.

minutes they soon found how criminally stupid such 'reports' were. Penny-Leigh and Elsdon realized they had little chance of mixing it with the Japanese and dived for home, but Stone, who had already won the DFC in France in 1940 for shooting down three German aircraft, unwisely stayed to fight. His notes made at the time graphically describe the one-sided combat: 'The first burst from one of the fighters tore a hole in my starboard long-range tank. Lucky it was not tracer. Another burst knocked away the starboard aileron. By this time the ten Army Type 97 fighters were queuing up to shoot at me, some performing remarkably accurate full-deflection shooting, their bullets making a twanging noise as they hit my Hurricane. I never had a chance to even fire my guns so manoeuvrable were my antagonists. For one awful moment I panicked and death appeared very close. I recovered myself and climbed straight into the sun, stall turned out of it, not daring to spin, and dived down among shipping in the estuary below, to make a somewhat shaky landing on the field. Sergeant Tug Wilson came up, and seeing the guns were not fired and the shambles the aircraft was in, merely turned around and walked away. His back expressed unmistakable disgust.'

This particular Hurricane was so badly damaged that it never flew again and was scrapped. But the following day Stone had his revenge and the disgust, or perhaps disappointment of the frustrated Sgt. Wilson, was forgotten. The only early-warning radar at Rangoon detected a large formation of hostile aircraft approaching, and No. 67 Sqn's. remaining Buffaloes, the AVG and the two remaining Hurricanes of No. 17 Sqn. took off to counter the threat. Flying Hurricane BG853 with Elsdon as his wingman, Stone climbed to 15,000 feet; this time a lot quicker as the offending tanks had been removed. Approaching from the south-east were seven Ki-21-1a's whose escort was being engaged by the P-40s of the AVG. Once again Sqn. Ldr. Stone's account of the action illustrates what happened: 'I went in from the sun and took the far one to allow the others room. My first burst set his starboard engine on fire, and he slowly dropped back with pieces falling off. As he turned away from the other bombers, a No. 67 Sqn. Buffalo appeared from nowhere, and fired a burst into the stricken *Sally*, which promptly blew up.

'My No. 2 (Jimmy Elsdon) had his engine hit, and with a dead propeller turned for Mingladon, which he succeeded in making. Meanwhile I went in again on two bombers which continued to fly serenely on. My eight Brownings responded magnificently and one bomber started to shed pieces as my ammunition found its mark. I turned my attention to his companion, who immediately started to stream petrol and commenced a slow spiral descent. By this time I was too close to continue firing and continued my dive through the formation only to be confronted by a Ki-27a *Nate* coming at me head-on.

'We both fired at each other and missed. I wondered

A well-chaperoned C-47 of an unknown SEAC transport unit.

An interesting photograph believed to have been taken at a base in Ceylon, showing mainly Hellcats of 1839 Sqn. FAA and Vengeances, the latter being most unusual in having, in most cases, British Pacific Fleet style markings.

Photographed in Burma during 1944, this Spitfire Mk VIII of No. 273 Sqn. bears a non-standard size and style of fuselage roundel for the theatre.

which way he would break as I continued to fly towards him, being determined not to be the first to waver. The Japanese pilot lost his nerve first and broke over my Hurricane; I immediately reefed into a tight turn, only to find him facing me again. The Ki–27a was so quick that for a moment I wished I was back at the controls of a Gladiator, which I am sure could have more than held its own. The turning twisting fight continued until we both ran out of ammunition, whereupon I flew alongside him and put up two fingers in the well-known salute; to my surprise he responded in like manner and gave me a wide grin, before heading back to Thailand. So at least some of the Japs were human!'

None of the Japanese raiders reached Rangoon on that occasion, but Stone's Hurricane had its propeller hit and there were no proper tools with which to change it. The maintenance crews had a very bad time in trying to keep the aircraft flying, and it was only the co-operation of the local railway engineers, who fabricated various tools in their workshops, which kept the Hurricanes airborne. The general ground organization was a complete farce, with spares and tools from support depots never seeming to arrive when they were needed. Similarly, motor transport was almost non-existent and Stone had to scrounge what he could from local car dealers and the AVG, whom he helped in return by lending some of No. 17

Sqn's. ground crew.

The long-range tanks which nearly cost Sqn. Ldr. Stone his life on 23 January featured again a few days later when he was ordered to take No. 17 Sqn. to strafe the Japanese airfield at Bangkok. He pointed out to the station commander, Group Captain Seton Broughall, that even with precise dead reckoning the Hurricanes would only have about three minutes over the enemy airfield, and the long-range tanks necessary to reach Bangkok would, in any event, make the Hurricanes sitting targets for the Japanese fighters, which were certain to defend their base. Even if they survived combat with such a disadvantage, the chances of getting back were very remote. Headquarters persisted in their request, but agreed to let Stone take only pilots he selected; his choice was Sqn. Ldr. Carey of No. 135 Sqn. and one of No. 17 Sqn's. flight commanders. Then, someone in the chain of command quickly realized that there was every chance of losing three of the most experienced pilots then in Burma, and no more was heard about attacking Bangkok.

More Hurricanes began to arrive, as did No. 113 Sqn. with Blenheims. Strikes were continually made against the Japanese, but the odds were still stacked highly against the RAF, although it took a steady toll of the raiders.

On 27 January No. 17 Sqn., which had pilots trained in night flying, agreed to try night interception of bombers raiding Rangoon. Prior to this the AVG had tried to operate at night, using car headlights as a flare path, but had lost two aircraft. The Hurricane pilots had trained in England at night and sometimes in somewhat dubious flying conditions, so they had something of an advantage, which they quickly put to good use. In an attempt to save some aircraft from the attention of Japanese raids on airfields, several dispersal strips were hacked out of the paddy fields by civilian labourers led by a planter who had been a pilot in the RFC. These strips were all named after different brands of whisky in honour of the planter, who was a Scot. On the night of 27 January the AVG had dispersed its aircraft to 'Johnny Haig', leaving No. 17 Sqn. in sole occupation at Mingladon. Sqn. Ldr. Stone and Jimmy Elsdon were at readiness when warning of a raid came through. Both pilots immediately took off; Elsdon to patrol up to 20,000 feet and Stone above. Anti-aircraft fire and bomb flashes were seen, but the two Hurricane pilots could not find any trace of the raiders; then, just when all seemed lost, Stone saw what he first thought was a shooting star. But it was maintaining a steady course and as the Hurricane approached, the pilot made out the glow coming from four exhausts. The shooting star was in fact two Army Type 97 bombers in formation. As Sqn. Ldr. Stone moved in for the kill, one of the aircraft opened fire, indicating that at least one gunner was aware of the danger. The Hurricane pilot fired at the bomber and immediately the shooting from it stopped. A kick on the rudder and a touch of aileron lined up the other bomber and a burst from the Hurricane sent it into a vertical dive. The British fighter followed it down, firing all the time, until, flaming from end-to-end, it plunged into the Irrawaddy. On landing Sqn. Ldr. Stone discovered that Jimmy Elsdon in the other Hurricane had also located the two bombers and had just been about to open fire when tracer from Stone's

guns had passed over him and ripped into the Japanese bomber. The following day wreckage from both bombers was found in the river and the two British pilots were fêted throughout Rangoon and made the front page of the local paper.

Meanwhile No. 135 Sqn. was still awaiting arrival of its Hurricanes and the CO, eager to get into the action, persuaded No. 17 Sqn. to let him fly with them. On 28 January he flew an interception mission with No. 17 and shot down a *Nate* fighter.

By mid-February the Hurricanes of Nos. 17 and 135 Sqns.—and No. 67, which had given up its four remaining Buffaloes and moved to Toungoo—were taking a heavy toll of the Japanese, but it was clear that on the ground the fighting was going very much in favour of the invaders. The 17th Division had retreated nearly to the Sittang River, suffering heavy losses in the jungle fighting. The Japanese used small forces, which they landed behind the British, who, instead of staying put and trying to fight their way past the Japanese, retreated in an outflanking manoeuvre, the inevitable result being yet another infiltration by the Japanese behind them, and another retreat. These enemy tactics were eventually to be used very successfully by Orde Wingate and his famous Chindits during the advance back through Burma.

Believed to have been an aircraft of No. 28 Sqn., this Spitfire PR XI appears to have had its white SEAC wing markings overpainted. Individual letter is 'K' on both the Spitfire and the fuselage of the Curtiss fighter in the background, believed serialled AK572, in which case it is a Kittyhawk Mk I.

A late-comer to SEAC was the Mosquito, the type equipping several units in small numbers towards the end of the Far Eastern campaign. These three FB VIs were part of No. 84 Sqn.

As the British retreated, Blenheims escorted by Hurricanes bombed airfields now occupied by the Japanese bases which a few weeks before they themselves had been using. By 26 February Nos. 17 and 135 Sqns. between them could muster only twelve Hurricanes, which were in constant use strafing Japanese troops and barges, as well as being used as escort bombers and intercepting any enemy raids. At Mingladon on the afternoon of 26 February, Flt. Lt. 'Bush' Cotton, one of the No. 17 Sqn. flight commanders, took off alone in a partly unserviceable Hurricane to intercept a Japanese raid. The rest of Nos. 17 and 135 Sqns. were away on bomber escort duty at the time. From 18,000 feet Cotton saw twenty-four Japanese bombers drop their lethal loads on the airfield from which he had just taken off. Diving into the attack he shot down one bomber and damaged another before twelve escorting fighters arrived. Cotton broke off the engagement, but instead of returning to base, climbed to 24,000 feet to mount another attack on the enemy force. The Hurricane could climb much faster than the *Nate*, and on reaching height Cotton once again felt he had the advantage. Pushing the Hurricane into a wing-over, Cotton descended on the bomber's top cover, but to his horror saw one of the nimble Japanese fighters pull up until it was nearly vertical, whereupon it fired at point blank range. Machine-gun bullets from the fighter ripped through the side of the Hurricane, smashing Cotton's left leg just below the knee. Despite over 130 hits, nothing of great

mechanical importance had been hit, and the Hurricane responded to Cotton's aileron turn and dive to zero feet. On reaching the airfield he found that all the hydraulics were still working, and by jamming his right foot under the toe strap on the rudder bar was able to bring off a decent landing and taxi to dispersal. The ground crew, seeing no movement from the cockpit, rushed to the aircraft and found Cotton slumped across the controls. He was evacuated to Calcutta, and the Hurricane, which was beyond repair, was blown up with a hand grenade. Subsequent reports by pilots of the AVG who were also involved in the action seem to indicate that the fighter that had damaged Cotton's Hurricane had a retractable undercarriage, so it was more likely a Mitsubishi A6M2 *Zero*, rather than a *Nate* as mentioned in the pilot's combat report.

During the first two months of 1942 the Japanese mounted thirty-one raids against Rangoon, and made a concentrated effort to gain air superiority. They never achieved this in the way they had in Malaya, but as the army gave up ground the RAF was forced to retreat northwards with them as their airfields fell into enemy hands. On March 21 nine Blenheims escorted by ten Hurricanes attacked the airfield at Mingladon, now occupied by the Japanese, destroying sixteen aircraft on the ground and eleven in the air. In retaliation the enemy sent a force of 230 aircraft to eliminate the base at Magwe from which the British aircraft had operated. Some aircraft escaped the bombardment and flew to Akyab, where they too were subjected to three days of almost continual bombardment. The air defence of Burma was practically over; Rangoon had fallen on 8 March, and Japanese forces were on the Indian border. The coming of the monsoon

Mosquito FB VI TE650 of No. 47 Sqn. at Butterworth, Malaya, after a heavy landing. Note the black SEAC identification bands on silver finish.

halted all land advances and the Allies were now in a position to reinforce their land and air forces in India ready for a major counter-offensive.

During the retreat from Burma unarmed DC-2K aircraft of No. 31 Sqn. performed a Herculean task in transporting reinforcements and stores into Burma and evacuating the injured. The DC-2s operated from Akyab until the bombing in March forced the squadron to move back into India, where they were located at Dum Dum.

In April the ageing DC-2s were supplemented by DC-3 Dakotas, three of which were detached to Dinjan, from where they dropped food and medical supplies on the major routes being used by evacuees from Burma. The aircraft were also used to remove military personnel, civilians and the wounded from Myitkyina to Dinjan.

In May No. 31 Sqn's. base at Myitkyina suffered heavy bombardment, but despite this and appalling weather the crews continued to operate, sometimes flying as many as five sorties a day. On some occasions, such as that on 6 May, tragedy struck. Two DC-3s were attacked by Japanese bombers just after they landed, women and children on board were killed and the survivors machine-gunned as they ran from the aircraft. During the retreat from Burma No. 31 Sqn. brought out over 4,000 men, women and children, in addition to carrying out various supply drops.

Throughout the rest of the war in this theatre the squadron repeatedly broke its own records for hours flown in support of the ground forces, and performed some remarkable feats of airmanship, including the landing by F/Off. M. Vlasto in a very restricted jungle clearing to rescue wounded Chindits. On many occasions No. 31 Sqn. accurately dropped supplies in very small dropping zones.

Transport aircraft and their crews often do not receive the full credit they deserve, but there can be no doubt that the efforts made by No. 31 Sqn. typify the air support so essential in any campaign, and especially that in Burma.

The Road Back

With the British forces pushed out of Malaya and Burma and similar successful campaigns in the Pacific completed, the Japanese had by mid-1942 gained domination of a huge slice of eastern Asia. Their 'empire' extended to the Solomon Islands in the east, to the Indian border in the west, Manchuria in the north and Java in the south. The territory they now occupied had been gained against numerically superior forces, of which over 300,000 had been captured; close on a million tons of shipping, including six battleships, had been sunk; 4,000 guns, 1,500 tanks and 240 aircraft had been captured. Against a loss of just over 600 Army and Navy aircraft could be credited the destruction of over 3,000 Allied aircraft, including the almost total annihilation of the RAF. The Japanese forces which had achieved this resounding success were not particularly powerful, but they had been well prepared and equipped and had struck at a time when the Allies had not been in a strong enough position to send sufficient reinforcements. In many ways the first six months of the war saw the Japanese reach a zenith of achievement that under close scrutiny indicates a false sense of proportion

Not all aircraft in SEAC markings were of a warlike variety; this Harvard was used by one of the training schools in India, its silver finish and large-size serial FX499 possibly indicating a post-war photograph.

when all factors of the various campaigns are analysed on equal merit.

Nevertheless, reinforcements started to arrive in quantity and Hurricanes of Nos. 30, 258 and 261 Sqns., supported by Fulmars of the Fleet Air Arm, were instrumental in beating off the attack by Admiral Naguma's carrier force on the island of Ceylon. The first attack on Colombo came on 5 April, when aircraft from five Japanese carriers attempted to carry out a surprise attack on the harbour as they had done at Pearl Harbor. No. 258 Sqn. took on the bombers and destroyed four enemy aircraft as well as damaging several others, but lost nine Hurricanes when they were caught by the escorting *Zeros*. No. 30 Sqn., which was taking off just as the first bombs fell, fared a little better, accounting for eleven enemy aircraft certainly destroyed and seven probables against a loss of eight Hurricanes and five pilots.

Four days later, carrier-borne aircraft struck again This time No. 261 Sqn., which had arrived at China Bay in March, shot down seven of the raiders for the loss of three pilots. In the two raids forty British fighters were lost, and the cruisers *Cornwall* and *Dorsetshire* were sunk, but although it looked to be yet another victory for the Japanese, and indeed was acclaimed as such by them, no ground was gained and the defenders had not suffered crippling casualties. This was in fact the last measure of

any real success the Japanese Navy was to enjoy, and it served only to produce a feeling of invincibility among its naval commanders, which led them to grossly underestimate the potential of the Allied naval forces.

Three of the carriers involved in the action off Ceylon had to return to Japan to refit and were therefore unable to take part in the decisive Battle of the Coral Sea, but perhaps of more importance was the fact that many of the pilots had been in action since the outbreak of war and those who still survived were becoming very battle weary. Those killed represented some of the most experienced aircrew available, and later, at the Battle of Midway, when the Japanese lost four carriers and saw the balance of naval power turn against them, they were sorely missed.

In India the task of rebuilding both land and air forces came under the auspices of the new Supreme Commander Far East Forces, General Sir Archibald Wavell, who arrived fresh from his success in North Africa in March 1942. His air commander was Air Chief Marshal Sir Richard Peirse, whose initial task was to reinforce his depleted squadrons, especially the fighters, to thwart any threat of strategic bombing against the industrial centres around Bengal. At the same time he had to establish bases from which new squadrons could operate and have their aircraft maintained. Early-warning radar units were set up in India and were soon operative, giving defending Hurricanes adequate warning of the few sporadic raids the Japanese mounted in April 1942. These gradually petered out, and throughout the spring and summer air activity was minimal, with the expected major thrust from the Japanese never coming.

continued on page 34

Disembarked from their parent carriers on 20 March 1945, Seafires of 807 and 809 Sqns. Royal Navy, part of No. 4 Fighter Wing, flew with Far East Air Force's Spitfire squadrons to gain operational experience of strike and tactical reconnaissance sorties over jungle terrain. Here machines of 807 Sqn. form a backdrop to armourers belting 20mm cannon ammunition at Katukurunda. The code of 807 was 'D5' split by the fuselage roundel and aircraft 'Y' and 'Q' can be seen. (Via L. Beckford)

Nice detail view of RN armourers fitting a 250lb bomb to the centre-line rack of a Seafire III at Katukurunda. (Via L. Beckford)

Page 25 above: Bristol Blenheim Mk I, L1134 of No. 62 Sqn., Alor Star, Kadah Province, December 1941. After a single-handed attack on Singora airfield on 9 December, this aircraft returned to base with the pilot, Acting Sqn. Ldr. A. K. S. Scarf, mortally wounded; he was awarded a posthumous VC on 21 June 1946. Shown in the finish carried at the time of the 1941 action, the aircraft has dark earth/dark green camouflage with black undersides. Type A1 roundels of 45.5in diameter appeared on the fuselage, with Type A 35in on upper and lower wing surfaces. The fin flash was 27 × 24in, with 8in serial and 2ft high code letters.
Below: Ground crew pause for the camera during servicing of a No. 28 Sqn. Hurricane Mk IIc in Burma.

Page 26 above: Westland Lysander T1688 of No. 357 Sqn. at Drigh Road, July 1945. This particular aircraft was flown by F/Off. H. V. D. Hallet and the unit was formed to support Force No. 136; colour details include green/grey camouflage, black undersides and yellow spinner. (H. V. D. Hallet via J. R. B. Edwards)
Below: Hawker Hurricane Mk IIb, BE171 of No. 17 Sqn., Mingladon, 1942. One of the first Hurricanes in Burma, this machine was flown by Wg. Cdr. C. A. C. Stone on the night of 27 January when he destroyed a Mitsubishi Ki-21 1a over Rangoon, the outer pair of the original twelve .303in Browning guns being removed. Aircraft shown in Scheme A camouflage with Sky Type S undersides; 35in diameter fuselage roundels and 45in Type A on wing upper surfaces; 27 × 24in fin flash, 8in serial and 2ft high codes.

Page 27 above: Bristol Beaufighter TF Mk X, RD 367, of No. 27 Sqn., 1945. Finished in ocean grey/dark green camouflage with medium sea grey undersides, this aircraft bore white SEAC identity bands as shown; the single code letter was 2ft high.
Below: Pleasing in-flight view of a Boeing-built Catalina IVB serialled JX431 and carrying the individual code 'A' on the fin, although the actual unit to which it belonged is unknown.

Pages 28–29: Republic Thunderbolt Mk I FL792 of No. 258 Sqn., Yelahanka, 1944. Finished in dark earth/dark green camouflage with light grey undersides, the aircraft has the nose chequers adopted by No. 258 for identification purposes. Fuselage codes were 18in high and all roundels of 16in diameter; fin flash dimensions were specified as 2ft × 2ft 3in.

Page 30 above: Consolidated Liberator B. Mk IV, EW267, of No. 355 Sqn., Salbani, late 1944–45. Shown in the American olive drab and neutral grey shades retained by most RAF Liberators in SEAC, the machine bears squadron identity markings on its rudders, a practice followed by at least four Liberator units in the theatre. The emblem appeared on the port side only and roundel dimensions were 25in on the wings and 36in on the fuselage, the fin flash, of 2ft × 2ft 3in, being applied to all four fin surfaces.
Below: The purposeful contours of a Spitfire XIV at Donmuang, Thailand, after the war. (L. Manwaring)

Page 31 above: (A) Palm tree insignia, No. 135 Sqn. (B) Ace of Spades insignia, No. 81 Sqn., shown on NMF. (C) Tail marking No. 356 Sqn. Liberator. (D) Tail marking, No. 215 Sqn. Liberator. (E) Tail marking, No. 99 Sqn. Liberator. (F) Nose marking, Thunderbolt of No. 134 Sqn. (G) insignia of No. 132 Sqn., Spitfire XIV. (H) Mailed fist insignia of No. 17 Sqn., Spitfire XIV. (I) Nose marking of Liberator B. Mk VI KH108, believed to have been part of No. 355 Sqn.
Below: Willys Jeep used by No. 17 Sqn., Burma 1942. It was found, along with other American vehicles, in a Burmese garage, and appropriately painted for squadron use.

Page 32: (1) Squadron Leader, Hurricane pilot, 1944. He wears army issue jungle green cellular shirt and slacks, standard issue Type C flying helmet with oxygen mask/microphone, and army issue webbing belt with revolver holster and ammunition pouch of 1937 pattern. The only insignia worn are the rank tabs slipped over the shirt shoulder straps—one thin between two thick stripes, light blue on dark blue.
(2) RAF groundcrew, 1944. The early part of the Far East war was characterized by use of khaki drill clothing and pith helmet. In 1943–45, cellular jungle green clothing of similar cut was issued and the Australian-style bush hat in khaki felt was worn, often with an RAF flash on the puggri in dark blue, light blue and dark red. On tropical uniform, both KD and jungle green, shoulder and trade insignia were worn in red on a KD background. Light jungle boots are worn, in a brown suede-finish leather.
(3) Deputy Provost Marshal, 1945, taken from a photograph of an officer in Rangoon. The jungle green shirt and slacks are worn with the blue-grey RAF sidecap. The latter bears the gilt crowned albatross badge on the left side, well forward, and two gilt buttons on the front of the flap. Rank tabs are slipped over the shirt shoulder straps—here, those of a flight lieutenant, two equal bars—and the felt brassard of this appointment is worn on the right arm. Standard 1937-pattern web pistol belt and holster are worn.

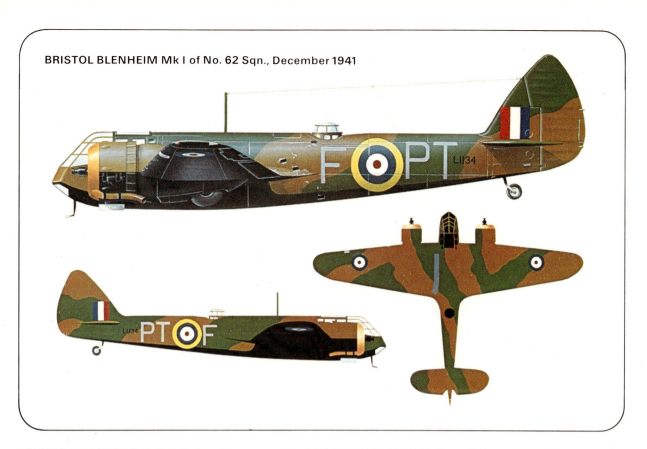

BRISTOL BLENHEIM Mk I of No. 62 Sqn., December 1941

HAWKER HURRICANE Mk IIb of No. 17 Sqn., 1942

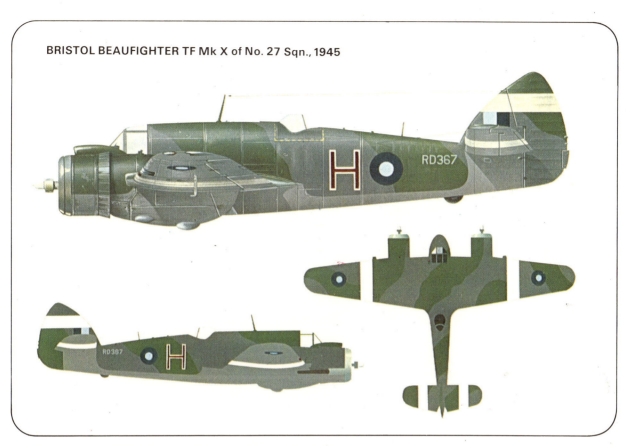

BRISTOL BEAUFIGHTER TF Mk X of No. 27 Sqn., 1945

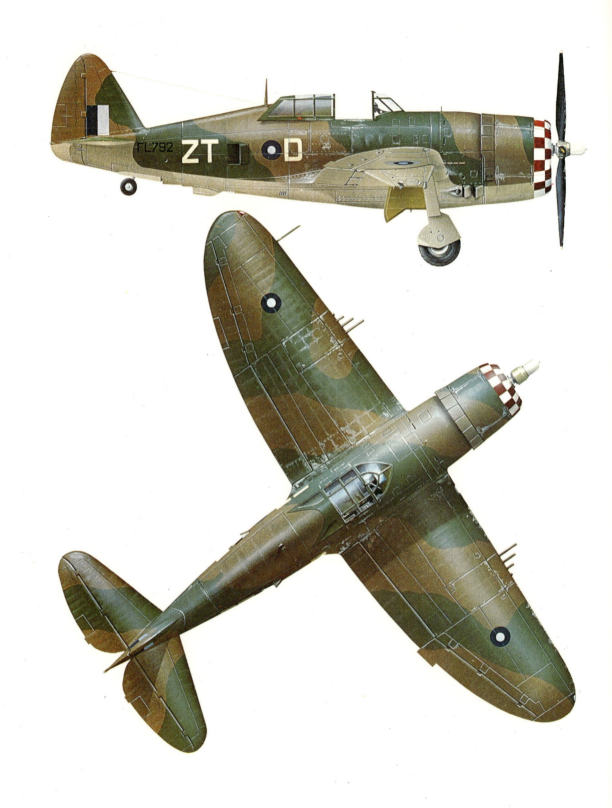

REPUBLIC THUNDERBOLT Mk I of No. 268 Sqn., 1944

CONSOLIDATED LIBERATOR B. Mk IV of No. 355 Sqn., 1944–45

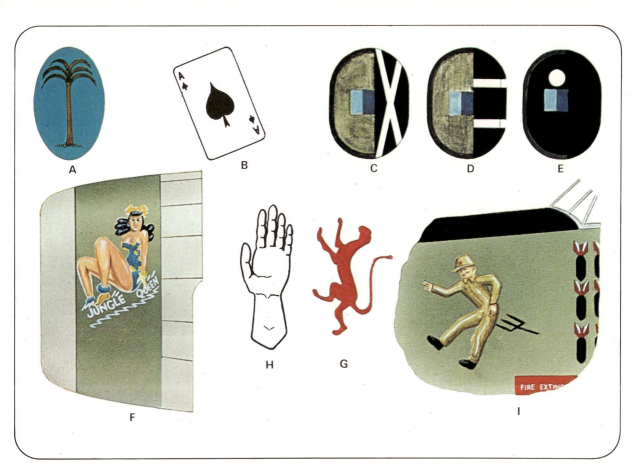

A   B   C   D   E

F   H   G   I

RAF BOMBER SQUADRONS, FAR EAST COMMAND 7 DEC. 1941

Malaya

Sqn.	Location	Aircraft
34	Tengah	Blenheim IV
60 (Det)	Kuantan	Blenheim I
62	Alor Star	Blenheim I

Burma

60	Mingladon	Blenheim I

RAF FIGHTER SQUADRONS, FAR EAST COMMAND 7 DEC. 1941

Malaya: Singapore Island

Sqn.	Location	Aircraft
PR Flight	Seletar	Buffalo
453 (RAAF)	Sembawang	Buffalo
21 (RAAF)	Sembawang	Buffalo
243	Kallang	Buffalo
488	Kallang	Buffalo

Mainland

27	Sungei Patani	Blenheim IF

RAF BOMBER SQUADRONS, INDIA JULY 1943

No. 221 Group

Sqn.	Location	Aircraft
45	Digri	Vengeance
82	Salbani	Vengeance
110	Digri	Vengeance
159	Salbani	Liberator II
42	Kumbhirgram	Blenheim V
99	Jessore	Wellington Ic
215	Jessore	Wellington Ic

No. 224 Group

11	Feni	Blenheim IV
113	Feni	Blenheim V

No. 225 Group

34	Yelahanka	Blenheim IV
60	Madras	Blenheim IV

AHQ Ceylon

84	Ratmalana	Vengeance

RAF FIGHTER SQUADRONS SOUTH-EAST ASIA 1 JULY 1944

No. 222 Group

Sqn.	Location	Aircraft
17	Vavuyina	Spitfire VIII
89	Vavuyina	Beaufighter VIF
176 (Det)	Vavuyina	Beaufighter VIF
273	Ratmalana	Spitfire VIII
176 (Det)	Ratmalana	Beaufighter VIF
135	Minneriya	Thunderbolt I

221 Group

60	Agartala	Hurricane IIc
81	Khumbirgram	Spitfire VIII
11	Lanka	Hurricane IIc
42	Kangla	Hurricane IV
176 (Det)	Kangla	Beaufighter VIF
113	Palel	Hurricane IIc
615	Palel	Spitfire VIII
152	Palel	Spitfire VIII
607	Imphal Main	Spitfire VIII
20 (Det)	Imphal Main	Hurricane IIc/IId
34	Dergaon	Hurricane IIc
60 (Det)	Dergaon	Hurricane IIc

No. 225 Group

5	Vizagapatam	Hurricane IIc
27	Cholavarum	Beaufighter VIF

No. 224 Group

136	Chittagong	Spitfire VIII
60 (Det)	Chittagong	Hurricane IIc
20	Chiringa	Hurricane IIc/IId
152	Palel	Spitfire VIII

Eastern Air Command

67	Baigachi	Spitfire VIII
155	Baigachi	Spitfire VIII
176	Baigachi	Beaufighter VIF
89 (Det)	St Thomas Mount	Beaufighter VIF
135 (Det)	Amarda Road	Thunderbolt Mk I

RAF BOMBER SQUADRONS, SEAC DECEMBER 1944

No. 231 Group

Sqn.	Location	Aircraft
159	Digri	Liberator VI
215	Digri	Liberator VI
355	Salbani	Liberator VI
356	Salbani	Liberator VI
99	Dhubalia	Liberator VI

No. 221 Group

45	Kumbhirgram	Mosquito VI
82	Kumbhirgram	Mosquito VI

Nose art, No. 358 Sqn. style on Liberator IV 'Q for Queenie'.

'The Woodcutter' was also a machine of No. 358 Sqn., carrying the code 'W'.

Peirse and his administration officer, Air Vice-Marshal A. C. Collier, reorganized their command, forming No. 222 Group at Colombo to look after the Indian Ocean, No. 221 Group at Calcutta with the task of carrying out all bombing and reconnaissance operations and No. 224 Group with a mandate for fighter operations. These three groups formed the main fighting elements of the RAF and were supported by No. 226 Group, a maintenance unit which handled most of the reinforcements flown into India, and No. 227 Group, based at Lahore to undertake training.

Set-backs in the Middle East caused some delays in aircraft reaching the Far East, but by the middle of 1942 eight squadrons were equipped with Hurricanes and the three light bomber squadrons evacuated from Burma had received new Blenheims. By the end of the year the total aircraft strength available to Peirse amounted to 1,443 among which were some photographic reconnaissance Spitfires and the nucleus of a night-bombing force in the form of Wellingtons.

In Calcutta the threatened air raids had never materialized and Hurricane pilots of No. 17 Sqn. enjoyed the use of the Grand Hotel as their readiness room—a far cry from the primitive conditions they had endured as they retreated across Burma. The hotel was only a short distance from the squadron's improvised runway, which was in fact the Governor's Drive through the Maidan (Park) of Calcutta, the colour of the drive surface soon leading to the pilots naming their runway 'The Red Road'. 'Bush' Cotton—now recovered from the leg wound received in combat with a *Zero*—returned to the squadron as a flying officer, having lost his temporary rank of flight-lieutenant during hospitalization. He recalls that it was fascinating taking off from 'The Red Road', which was steeply cambered and not as wide as it at first appeared. The marble balustrades on either side were adorned with statues and there was an air of unreality as the Hurricanes darted between them before becoming airborne and climbing away between city buildings from whose

A group of No. 135 Sqn. Thunderbolt pilots wearing a wide variety of flying clothing and headgear. (Via L. Hawkins)

windows pretty office girls would wave at the pilots. By the end of December Cotton's rank had been restored and he was now OC 'A' Flight, but there was a distinct lack of action, that occurring being mainly abortive attempts at night interception of a few desultory raids.

The commanders of the Japanese air force were subordinate to the army, which did not support strategic bombing, a fact highlighted by the lack of concentration on this form of attack. But in December Calcutta was bombed at night. Little material damage was caused, but the population panicked and a mass exodus began.

Peirse needed radar-equipped night fighters to counter this development and these arrived on 13 January 1943 from the Middle East in the form of three Beaufighters of No. 89 Sqn. These aircraft became the nucleus of the second Beaufighter squadron to arrive in the theatre, the first being No. 27 Sqn., which took its new aircraft into action on Christmas Eve, when Wg. Cdr. H. Daish led five aircraft in an attack on Toungoo airfield.

No. 358 Sqn's. Liberators lined up at Digri, with 'The Woodcutter' nearest the camera. The squadron carried out one bombing raid on Mandalay on 13 January 1945 and then became a special duties unit, dropping supplies and agents behind Japanese lines. The photograph probably shows the aircraft being prepared for this role, as the nearest two have their top turrets removed and 'W' appears to be in the process of having its paint stripped back to NMF.

Well-marked Spitfire XIVe was RN135 of No. 17 Sqn., flown by the CO, Sqn. Ldr. J. H. 'Ginger' Lacey, from Seletar in 1945. The white codes are outlined in black and the unit's mailed fist badge appears under the exhausts. Adjacent to the cockpit is a squadron leader's pennant and 27 German crosses, reflecting the pilot's previous service in Europe. The single Japanese kill dates this photograph as later than 19 February 1945, the date of Lacey's 28th and last victory of the war.

Thunderbolt II KL314 of No. 258 Sqn. NMF aircraft had their SEAC bands in black or medium blue—which appears to be the case with this particular machine.

Two days after their arrival the three Beaufighters, now part of No. 176 Sqn. under the command of Wg. Cdr. J. A. O'Neill, were called into action from Dum Dum when warning was received of an approaching raid. The first air-to-air combat between the powerful twin-engined night fighter and Japanese Army Air Force Type 97 bombers resulted in a convincing victory for the British machine. Beaufighter X7776 with Flt. Sgt. A. Pring at the controls and Sgt. C. Phillips as his radar operator, shot down three of the raiders in the space of four minutes; these three added to three previous victories in Egypt immediately elevated Pring to the ranks of the 'aces' as well as bringing an immediate award of the DFM. On 19 January the squadron suffered its first casualty, when F/Off. C. Crombie, an Australian pilot, intercepted another formation of Army Type 97 bombers. This time the Japanese gunners were alert and their defensive fire set the Beaufighter's starboard engine on fire. Crombie accounted for one bomber before ordering his observer to bale out, shot down another and was in the process of attacking a third when the Beaufighter blew up, forcing him to use his parachute to escape. This action resulted in the award of a DSO to Crombie, and brought the short series of night raids on Calcutta to an end. It was almost a year before the Japanese again turned their attention to the city, and sadly one of the victims was Flt. Sgt. Pring, who was shot down

in a Hurricane as he tried to intercept a daylight raid on the morning of 6 December 1943.

As the RAF in Burma was being rebuilt, throughout the summer months of 1942 attention was also being directed to strengthen the defence of the Australian continent, which was now within comparatively easy striking range of Japanese air forces.

Most of the Royal Australian Air Force's front-line fighter strength had been destroyed in the defence of Singapore, and the anticipated cover of her northern seaboard by units of the US Navy's Pacific Fleet had disappeared in the destruction at Pearl Harbor. Concerned at the possibility of Japanese landings in the Darwin area, the Australian government turned to the British for help, requesting the transfer of Spitfires to the now undefended area. Aircraft from a Japanese carrier force had raided Darwin on 19 February, during which ten USAAF P-40s, which attempted to defend the area, were destroyed. Another air raid on 3 March, which had gone unmolested, served to highlight the potentially dangerous situation. There was, therefore, great relief when Winston Churchill agreed to send three squadrons of the requested Spitfires to support the three units of the USAAF 49th Fighter Group, which had arrived in March.

The squadrons chosen were Nos. 452 and 457, both manned by Australians, and No. 54 Sqn. All three left the UK in March and on arrival in Australia formed No. 1 Fighter Wing. Various delays occurred in providing the squadrons with their Spitfire Vc's and it was not until January 1943 that the first patrols were flown. On 6 February No. 54 Sqn. had the honour of claiming the first

victory by an Australian-based Spitfire when Flt. Lt. R. Foster, flying Mk Vc BS181, shot down a Mitsubishi Ki 46 *Dinah*. Almost exactly one month later an Australian pilot of No. 457 Sqn., Flt. Lt. Maclean, opened his unit's account with the destruction of another *Dinah*. March saw considerable activity on the part of the Japanese bomber force with the biggest raid coming on the 15th, when a force of 22 medium bombers with a strong fighter escort attacked Darwin. The third squadron that formed No. 1 Fighter Wing, No. 452, was in action for the first time on that day, shooting down a Mitsubishi G4M *Betty* bomber and a *Zero*, but losing its CO, Sqn. Ldr. R. Thorold-Smith, in the process. That loss was more than avenged by No. 54 Sqn., pilots of which shot down three *Zeros* and a *Betty* for the loss of two pilots. Raids on Darwin and various airfields continued until 6 July, when the Japanese abandoned their aerial attacks against the Australian mainland.

During the major raids in May to July, the Spitfires shot down thirty-four enemy aircraft and lost twelve of their own aircraft in air-to-air combats, which in many ways were the closest in the Far East campaign to those fought over England during the Battle of Britain.

By March 1944 Spitfire VIIIs had replaced the ageing Mk Vs, and Nos. 452 and 457 Sqns. soon moved on to New Guinea, where they became part of the RAAF's 1st Tactical Air Force, their place in Australia being taken by Nos. 548 and 549 Sqns. These three squadrons took part in '*Rhubarbs*' against Japanese bases and installations, but in most cases the ranges involved were too great for Spitfires, so the rest of their war was spent on defensive patrols, and at readiness for raids that never materialized.

The 'Ace of Spades' insignia of No. 81 Sqn. was 'borrowed' from JG 53, the German fighter *Geschwader* that had opposed it in North Africa. This Thunderbolt II carries the widely applied badge on green and brown camouflage finish.

By December 1942 Wavell felt that he had strong enough land and air forces to mount an offensive the objective of which was the recapture of Akyab. Thus, led by Lieutenant-General N. Irwin, the army left Cox's Bazaar on 16 December and eleven days later had advanced well down the Mayu Peninsula to Indin, where it awaited fresh supplies. But the Japanese managed to reinforce their garrison at Akyab as well as moving troops into the Kaladan Valley on Irwin's left flank. The army held on until April then retreated, bringing to a premature end what has become known as the first Arakan campaign. But many valuable lessons had been learned as far as air support was concerned. Wavell knew that air superiority was an absolute necessity, and this first campaign went a long way to proving that the RAF was strong enough to sweep the Japanese air forces from the skies. Hurricane fighter bombers had now replaced Blenheims in some of the bomber squadrons and they were used to great effect in attacking Japanese land forces with bombs and machine-gun fire. Beaufighters, with their heavier firepower and greater range, were also beginning to make their presence felt, although at this time their numbers were still comparatively few when compared with Hurricanes.

In February Beaufighters of No. 27 Sqn. were in action on many occasions, their tasks varying from coastal patrols to strikes against enemy transport barges on the Chindwin River and enemy airfields. At this time the squadron was operating from Agartala, a base it shared with No. 5 Sqn., which was flying Curtiss Mohawk fighters. During the month No. 27 lost two aircraft during attacks on Heho and Frome airfields and in March two more Beaufighters were shot down, the second of these on one of the rare occasions when Japanese fighters intervened.

On 4 April No. 27 Sqn. experienced a repeat of its early days in Malaya when a Japanese force caught it on the ground at Agartala. Eighteen Army Type 97 bombers escorted by *Zeros* dropped high-explosive bombs on the airfield damaging two Beaufighters, destroying buildings and causing heavy casualties among Indian workers and other civilians. This raid did not cause the problems those of 1941 had, however, and in a very short space of time the Beaufighters were hitting back far into enemy-held territory. The range of the Beaus enabled them to venture far and wide into Burma, attacking fuel dumps, troop concentrations and, most important of all, the Japanese lines of communication. In April some aircrew members of No. 27 were posted to Pharpamau to form the nucleus of the forming No. 177 Sqn., which had originally arrived from Egypt in January but whose crews had operated with No. 27 due to a lack of their own aircraft. By the time replacement Beaufighters had arrived for them in May

Scourge of the Japanese, who dubbed it 'Whispering Death', the Beaufighter gave valuable service in the Far East, having both the range and firepower to give effective air support to ground forces. This one, a Mk X, was part of No. 22 Sqn., with white SEAC wing bands and abbreviated tail band. The aircraft carries a long-range fuel tank below the fuselage and RP rails under the wings.

many of the original crews had been lost, so crews from No. 27 Sqn. merged with the new crews and began working up to operational status, which they achieved in September.

The RAF's main base at Chittagong was a staging post for the Beaufighters, which used it as a refuelling stop before proceeding on their interdiction missions over the Burmese jungle, and it came as no surprise, therefore, when the Japanese turned their attention to it. One of the heaviest raids occurred in May, just prior to the army's final withdrawal from the Arakan, but the fighter strength that had been so lacking during the Malayan campaign was now a formidable force and the Japanese raiders suffered heavy casualties. Instrumental in training the Hurricane pilots was Wg. Cdr. Frank Carey, who had arrived in the theatre with No. 17 Sqn. in December 1941. As previously related, he had achieved his first victory with No. 17 Sqn. while waiting for No. 135's aircraft to arrive, and had commanded No.135 Sqn's. Hurricanes until February 1942. After this he moved to command the Air Fighting Training Unit at Calcutta, and during the May raid on Chittagong, now as a wing commander, he led the Hurricanes in the defence of the airfield. During this raid Carey's superb flying and gunnery was a lesson to his colleagues and he achieved the distinction of claiming a *Zero* without even firing his guns at it, the Japanese pilot flying into a hill while trying to emulate the British pilot's prowess. By the end of the war Carey's victory tally stood at twenty-eight, but many historians consider this to be a very conservative estimate.

During the abortive expedition into the Arakan another event had taken place which was to lay the foundations of a major contribution to final victory—Brigadier Orde

Wingate's first Chindit expedition deep into central Burma. The success of the 77th Brigade—the official name for the Chindits—depended entirely on air support and it was not let down by Nos. 31 and 194 Sqns., which, during the four-month campaign, flew 178 sorties, dropping over 300 tons of supplies. The Chindits' task was to infiltrate behind Japanese lines, destroying bridges, railway lines and generally undermining the morale of enemy troops, who until this time believed that only they had mastered this type of jungle warfare. The crews of the supply-dropping Dakotas were faced with tremendous difficulties in locating dropping zones and then accurately placing their vital loads within them. They rarely failed in these exacting tasks and on his return Wingate was full of praise for the fortitude and skills of the RAF transport crews.

In June 1943 the monsoon season curtailed most major air and land operations, although the RAF continued to fly some support missions and supply drops, the Dakotas being escorted by Hurricanes when flights over enemy territory were involved. The escorts were rarely needed, as enemy air activity was very slight, since by the end of May a considerable number of Japanese air force units in the area had been withdrawn to fronts which were under more severe pressure; at this time the American campaign in the Pacific was gathering momentum and resulted in a reduction of available front-line aircraft over Burma.

During the rainy season the build-up of RAF strength continued at a tremendous pace and by June, thirty-eight squadrons, of which seventeen were fighters and seven bombers, were operational. The establishment of such a powerful air force was guaranteed to give complete air superiority when the final bid for victory came.

Although later model Thunderbolt IIs equipped most RAF squadrons by 1945, some of the Mk Is soldiered on until the end. This example, in the hands of No. 113 Sqn., was seen at Ondaw in March 1945, coded 'GQ-R'.

The less glamorous tasks of artillery spotting, liaison and clandestine supply behind enemy lines were handled by light aircraft such as the Stinson L-5 Sentinel, 'Burma Belle' being one example.

Spitfire VIIIs of No. 132 Sqn. at dispersal at Kai Tak, Hong Kong. 'FF-B' RN133 has the name 'Jean VII' above the Squadron Leader's pennant and the unit badge, a rampant leopard, below the exhausts.

Burma Regained

Although numerically the Hurricane still represented the most widely available operational aircraft in India during 1943, and in fact still equipped some squadrons when final victory was achieved, new types were beginning to arrive during the first Arakan campaign. Most significant of these was the American-built Vultee Vengeance dive bomber, which went into action with No. 82 Sqn. on 17 November 1942, when shipping was attacked in the Bay of Bengal. These operations, which for a time were also carried out by No. 110 Sqn., came to a premature end, and it was not until March 1943 that the aircraft was used to actually bomb Japanese troops. The distinction of being the first squadron to operate the Vengeance against land targets fell to No. 110 Sqn., which despatched six aircraft on 19 March to attack a Japanese headquarters at Hitzwe.

Dive bombing was a technique new to RAF pilots, but once they had perfected it, they became expert at hitting their objectives with commendable precision. One of the shortcomings of the Vengeance was its inadequate defensive armament, but in April this was rectified by the installation of .303in Browning machine-guns in place of the original .30in American-manufactured Brownings, which were prone to jamming.

Nos. 45, 82, 84 and 110 Sqns. were equipped with the Vengeance and apart from No. 84 Sqn., which moved to Ceylon, were all in action during the first Arakan campaign. Most of their attacks were on Japanese troop concentrations in the jungle or at Akyab, but the monsoon severely curtailed operations and it was not until the second campaign was mounted that the aircraft really earned a name for itself in the close-support role.

One of the other important aircraft to arrive was the Spitfire, which, in Mk Vc form, began to equip Nos. 136, 607 and 615 Sqns. in December. Prior to this the only Spitfires operating in the area were photographic reconnaissance versions, but on many occasions rumours were rife that the fighter which had won such decisive victories in Europe would soon be arriving in the Far East. These rumours can be traced back to the early days of the campaign in Malaya, so it is not surprising that they were treated with contempt by veterans, who, no doubt, could hardly believe their eyes when the aircraft finally appeared. In retrospect it is perhaps fortunate that the Spitfire did not materialize in Malaya earlier. For although it was undoubtedly superior to the Hurricane in the air-to-air combat role, it was by no means as rugged, and the primitive airfields from which the RAF was operating in 1941–42 could well have taken a heavy toll of it.

During July 1943 Wellington B Mk X bombers started to arrive and equipped Nos. 99 and 215 Sqns., and the following month long-range Liberators helped the expansion of the bomber force, these being operated by Nos. 355 and 159 Sqns. The range of the Liberator III enabled the bomber force to venture across Burma and beyond to attack Japanese road and rail communication systems, one of the most noticeable trips being carried out by No. 159 Sqn., which flew a round trip of over 3,000 miles on 27-28 October 1944 to mine the approaches to Penang harbour.

Peel off by Vengeances of No. 12 Sqn. RAAF, code 'NH'.
The two aircraft in the background have white bars on the
elevators, which may have been sighting aids for the rear
gunner.

Manna from Heaven via Dakota was one of the most welcome sights to men of 14th Army.

The expansion of the air forces, which in November 1943 became South East Asia Command (SEAC), combining both the American and British air forces under one commander, meant that attention had to be given to the construction of airfields. Initially this was a slow task due to local conditions and the lack of machinery or skilled labour, but by the time SEAC came into existence, 275 airfields had been completed, some of them being hacked out of seemingly impossible bush country.

By December 1943, forty-nine RAF squadrons were operational and another twelve were in the process of working up; of these the transport units would play a vital part in the forthcoming campaign, as they were now able to carry whole divisions into action and keep them supplied with vital equipment.

The new Supreme Commander of SEAC was Vice-Admiral Lord Louis Mountbatten, the youngest Supreme Commander since Napoleon. His air commander was Air Chief Marshal Sir Richard Peirse, whose task was four-fold: (1) The destruction of the Japanese air force in Burma; (2) The defence of India; (3) Support of 14th Army, and (4) Support of Wingate's Chindits. To achieve these objectives the combined air forces were reorganized into three groups; a Tactical Air Force under Air Marshal Sir John Baldwin, a Strategic Air Force under Brigadier-General Howard Davidson of the USAAF, and a Troop Carrier Command under Brigadier-General D. Old.

With the force now at his disposal, Peirse felt confident that he could achieve the air superiority needed, and events were to prove him right. The Spitfire proved more than capable of handling anything the Japanese could put into the air against it and one of the immediate benefits gained was the cessation of enemy air reconnaissance, which had been carried out by Ki-46 *Dinah*s. These aircraft had been operating with impunity against the Hurricanes, but within a month of the Spitfire's arrival, four had been shot down, so photographic reconnaissance of the Allied build-up in the Arakan became a most difficult task for the Japanese. No. 136, one of the veteran squadrons which had been resting in India, returned with Spitfires to Chittagong in December 1943 and was immediately in action, destroying twelve enemy aircraft attempting to raid shipping off the Arakan coast on 31 December 1943, by which time the kill ratio in favour of the Spitfire was 8 to 1.

Preliminary moves by British forces down the west side of the Arakan Peninsula started in October 1943, and in the following three months the army began to appreciate the effect the Vengeance had on their advances. The dive bombers, escorted by Hurricanes or Spitfires, and frequently accompanied by Mohawks carrying small fragmentation bombs, were called in to clear the way for the advancing troops. Their targets ranged from villages where Japanese troops were known to be concentrated, to ammunition dumps and individual gun emplacements. The enemy air force at this time could muster some 200 fighters and 110 bombers in Burma, the remainder of its force of some 370 machines being scattered as far away as

Thailand, Indo-China, Malaya and Sumatra. Losses in air-to-air combat mounted at such a rate that reinforcements became vital, but in many cases movement of fighters simply left another door open through which SEAC could strike at vulnerable parts of the Japanese lines of communication. Such was the air superiority gained by Allied fighters that on many occasions there was no opposition from Japanese fighters and the Vengeances could operate quite comfortably without their escorts. But the Japanese were tenacious and did not easily give up ground they had captured. Official records quote many occasions where the army came to a halt in front of deeply entrenched Japanese strongholds which only capitulated under attack from Liberators, Wellingtons, USAAF Mitchells and the ubiquitous Vengeance, whose bombing accuracy often provided the 'straw which broke the camel's back'.

Losses to ground fire were quite considerable, not only in the Arakan but all over Burma, where Beaufighters, which had now been joined by a small force of Mosquitoes, continued to harry the Japanese wherever they could locate them or signs of their presence. Such losses were understandable since most of the operations involved extremely low-level flying across hostile jungle, from which there was little chance of escape in the event of a crash landing.

At the end of 1943 a four-pronged thrust into Burma began, supported by the Vengeance squadrons, which gave close support to the army, whilst the Wellingtons and Liberators made both night and day attacks on enemy airfields, roads, ports and railways. Some raids were directed against Rangoon and the Burma-Thailand road, as well as such distant targets as Moulmein and Bangkok.

On 3 February, the Japanese mounted a major counter-attack in the Arakan with the aim of penetrating deep into Assam and cutting the aerial supply route across the Himalaya mountains—known to the crews as 'the Hump'. But they made a serious miscalculation. Using the well-tried tactics employed during their advances in Malaya and Burma in 1942, they found to their surprise that this time the British did not retreat and allow themselves to be outflanked, but stayed put, dug-in, and continued to fight. At a small place called Sinzweya the army held fast against superior forces, its ability to do so being due to a continual supply of food, ammunition and equipment by Dakotas and C-46 Commando aircraft of the USAAF Troop Carrier Command, which were protected against considerable Japanese fighter activity by the ever-present Spitfires, which, during the seige, accounted for sixty enemy fighters.

By the end of April the first phase of the planned Japanese counter-offensive had failed, but it did not stop them from attempting a similar enterprise at Imphal. Fierce fighting at Imphal and Kohima was again supported

A Vultee Vengeance at Donmuang, Thailand, just after the war, showing the not uncommon second presentation of the serial number above the fin flash. (L. Manwaring)

This Thunderbolt II KL882/MU-H of No. 60 Sqn., was also pictured at Donmuang after the war. (L. Manwaring)

from the air both in terms of supply and support. Vengeances and Hurricanes continually harried the Japanese, aircraft sometimes being called in by army commanders to attack strongpoints which were only 100 yards in front of Allied positions. During these actions the aircraft would occasionally make low strafing runs or simulated attacks in which they neither dropped bombs nor fired their guns. The objective of these was to keep the Japanese in their foxholes whilst the infantry advanced on their positions and carried out the required devastation with bayonets: between March and June the Japanese lost 30,000 men in northern Burma in attempting to hold their positions or push the Allies off the Imphal plain. It was a lost cause and, as they retreated, Mountbatten gave them no respite. Once again the monsoon season started, but this time it did not cause a halt to be called. Whilst the army struggled through the dense jungle its vital air support continued to operate in most appalling weather, during which heavy rain and cloud bases of less than 200 feet created additional hazards for the pilots.

Between the two major Japanese offensives, another Chindit expedition had been mounted. A force of over 9,000 men, 1,100 mules and 175 ponies was carried over 150 miles behind the enemy lines by Dakotas and gliders, many of which landed on improvised landing strips hacked out of the jungle by engineers and troops. These strips were also used to evacuate the wounded by Stinson Reliant communication aircraft, whose pilots showed remarkable courage and skill in operating their light unarmed aircraft deep in Japanese-occupied territory. The Chindits created havoc behind the Japanese lines in much the same way as

the Long Range Desert Group had in the Middle East. Each Chindit column was accompanied by an RAF officer who liaised with patrolling aircraft: he called them in to bomb pockets of resistance, he directed medium bombers against their targets, and he chose areas where ambulance aircraft could land. By November 1944 the Japanese had been driven from the mountain areas, and the British army had crossed the Chindwin in three places, ready to advance through Mandalay to Rangoon.

Air Chief Marshal Sir Richard Peirse gave up his command on 26 November and his place was taken by Air Marshal Sir Guy Garrod, who stepped in when the originally named air commander, Air Chief Marshal Leigh-Mallory, was killed *en route* to take up his appointment. Garrod performed his caretaking role until February 1945, when Air Marshal Sir Keith Park took over the reins.

Although considerable credit must be given to the evergreen Hurricane, the fact that final air superiority in the straight fighter-versus-fighter role came only with the arrival of the Spitfire, especially the Mk VIII, must not be overlooked. Another aircraft which started to arrive in late 1943, but did not make its full impact until 1944, was the Republic Thunderbolt. This huge—compared with contemporary British fighters—aircraft was immediately popular with its RAF pilots, who did initially experience some difficulty with its speed, especially in the dive.

First to re-equip with the Thunderbolt Mk I was No. 135 Sqn., which began conversion in Ceylon in May 1944. But it was Nos. 146 and 261 Sqns. which first took the heavyweight fighter into action in September when they strafed enemy positions along the Chindwin. In October they were joined by Nos. 30, 135 and 258 Sqns., now part of No. 224 Group, which were also immediately in the fray, providing close support for 15 Corps. Such actions were rarely interfered with by the remaining Japanese air force fighters, but the enemy did try taking on the Thunderbolt when it was flown as close escort to Liberators. One such occasion was on 3 November, when Liberators attacked the Insein rail workshops near Rangoon, and No. 30 Sqn. engaged intercepting Nakajima Ki-44 *Tojo* fighters. The Thunderbolts disrupted the attack, destroying one of the *Tojos* before the Japanese pilots withdrew.

Although it could more than hold its own in the combat role, the Thunderbolt's major attribute was its 2,000lb bomb-carrying capacity and heavy firepower, both of which were time and time again forcibly demonstrated to ground troops who had called upon air support for help. The all-round versatility of the Thunderbolt is summed up by Sqn. Ldr. Hawkins, a former pilot of No. 17 Sqn., who also operated Hurricanes with No. 135 when it was the most forward RAF unit in the first Arakan offensive and flew its aircraft off beaches. Hawkins recounts how the Thunderbolt responded in the air to the most delicate touch, belying its rather cumbersome appearance on the ground—its fantastic acceleration in the dive; its steadiness as a gun platform; and, perhaps in many ways of most importance to its pilots, the amount of punishment it could absorb and still stay in the air.

Throughout 1944 and 1945, both the ground and air forces were faced with a hard fight against a fanatical enemy who did not have the word surrender in his vocabulary. The Japanese fought tenaciously in every situation, whether it be a whole division or just a patrol. But under inspired leadership and in ground conditions that at times were more taxing than anything the enemy could throw at them, the Allied armies relentlessly advanced, supported in every aspect by an air force that now completely dominated what had once been alien skies.

In January 1945 a fearsome new weapon joined those which were already rained on the unfortunate Japanese army, and the Thunderbolt delivered it. This weapon was

An abandoned Mitsubishi Ki-46 *Dinah*, typical of the many Japanese aircraft left on jungle airstrips in the Far East at the end of the war. One of the finest reconnaissance aircraft employed by any of the combatant nations, the Ki-46 posed the Allies a considerable interception problem.

The aircraft that more than any other was instrumental in early Japanese victories was the superlative Mitsubishi A6M *Zero-Sen*; this Model 21 of the Tainan Air Corps was one of the first more or less intact examples to be examined by the Allies. It was shot down over Port Moresby in July 1942.

napalm, a form of jellied petrol against which there was little defence and no cover. No. 135 Sqn. dropped its first load on Japanese positions near Kangaw on 29 January and The following day Nos. 5, 30, 123 and 258 Sqns. also used it to good effect on observation posts and bunkers.

Throughout the advance across Burma, Japanese airfields came in for the same treatment that had been meted out by their aircraft in 1942, and in many cases the fields concerned were those which had been occupied by the RAF during the whirlwind advance of the victorious Japanese army. But time was now running out and although spirited defence was encountered in almost every pocket of resistance, the end was in sight.

There was no let up by the Allies and in July all available airpower was called in to foil the last desperate Japanese attempt to retreat across the Sittang. In nine days of furious action, Spitfires, Thunderbolts, Beaufighters and Hurricanes continually harried the Japanese, flying over 3,000 sorties, during which they killed 10,000 enemy troops. Two years before the British army had suffered a heavy defeat on the banks of the same river; those casualties were now well and truly avenged.

Mandalay fell on 20 March, and Rangoon was retaken on 3 May; by the end of July the Japanese had been swept out of Burma, and attention now had to be turned to Malaya, Singapore and Japan itself.

Plans were well in hand to add even more strength to the SEAC air forces; a strategic bomber offensive was to be carried out by Lancasters of 'Tiger Force', the ranks of which included many veterans of Bomber Command who had learned their trade in the skies over Germany. But in August two mushroom-shaped clouds billowed over Hiroshima and Nagasaki, bringing in their wake an unconditional surrender by the Japanese, as well as a new dimension to warfare, which was to have far-reaching effects on every type of conflict in the following decades.

*   *   *

Among the many types used for communications and liaison duties in SEAC was the Beech Expeditor, an uncamouflaged example of which was seen at Donmuang after the war. (L. Manwaring)

'A' Flight of No. 110 Sqn. posing with one of the unit's Vengeance dive bombers, which has the upper and lower wing dive brakes fully extended. (N. H. Lambert)

Specifications, Main Types

Brewster Buffalo
Span 35ft, *length* 26ft, *weight empty* 4,479lb, *weight loaded*
6,840lb. *Powerplant* Wright Cyclone 1,100hp GR-1820-G
105a. *Armament* Four .50 or .303 machine-guns in wings and
fuselage. *Max. speed* 292mph at 20,000ft, *cruising speed*
255mph. *Service ceiling* 30,500ft.

Republic P-47D Thunderbolt
Span 40ft 9¼in, *length* 36ft 1¾in, *weight empty* 10,000lb, *weight
loaded* 14,600lb. *Powerplant* Pratt and Whitney double Wasp
2,300hp R-2, 800-59 radial. *Armament* Eight .50in machine-
guns. Bomb load 2,000lb. *Max. speed* 427mph. *Service ceiling*
36,500ft.

Vultee Vengeance
Span 48ft, *length* 40ft, *weight loaded* 12,840lb. *Powerplant*
Wright Double Row Cyclone 1,700hp GR 2600-A5B-5 radial.
Armament Four .30 machine-guns in wings and twin .30 or
.303 in rear cockpit. Bomb load 2,000lb. *Max. speed* 279mph,
cruising speed 250mph. *Service ceiling* 24,300ft.

Spitfire Mk VIII (typical)
Span 40ft 2in, *length* 31ft 3½in, *weight loaded* 7,767lb. *Max.
weight* 8,000 lb. *Powerplant* Rolls-Royce Merlin 1565hp type
61. *Armament* Two 20mm cannon and four .303 machine-guns,
or four 20mm cannon and 1,000lb bombs. *Max. speed* 408 mph
at 25,000ft. *Service ceiling* 44,000ft.

Sqn. Ldr. L. Hawkins of No. 135 Sqn. on the wing of his
Thunderbolt Mk I, showing well how the four .50 cal.
machine-guns were set horizontally rather than following
the dihedral angle. (L. Hawkins)

Notes sur les planches en couleur

Page 25 dessus: Bristol Blenheim Mk I, L1134 de No. 62 Sqn., Alor
Star, Kadah Province, décembre 1941. Illustré dans le fini porte en temps
de combat de 1941, cet avion tient camouflage brun foncé/vert foncé avec
côtés de dessous noires.

Dessous: Personnel rampant s'arrête pour l'appareil pendant entretien
d'un No. 28 Sqn. Hurricane Mk IIc en Burma.

Page 26 dessus: Westland Lysander T1688 de No. 357 Sqn. à Drigh
Road, juillet 1945. Cet avion particulier fut volé d'officier aviateur
H. V. D. Hallet et la fraction fut formée pour soutenir Force No. 136;
détails en couleur comprennent camouflage vert/gris, côtés de dessous
noires et fileur jaune.

Dessous: Hawker Hurricane Mk IIb, BE171 de No.17 Sqn., Mingladon,
1942. Un des premiers Hurricanes en Birmanie, cet appareil est illustré en
camouflage *Scheme A* avec côtés de dessous *Sky Type S*; rondelles sur
fuselage de 35in diamètre et 45in *Type A* sur les hautes surfaces d'escadre
27 × 24in écusson sur dérive, 8in lettres de série et chiffre 2ft en hauteur.

Page 27 dessus: Bristol Beaufighter TF Mk X, RD515, de No. 22 Sqn.,
1945. Fini en camouflage de couleurs grise d'océan/verte foncée avec
côtés de dessous grises de mer moyennes, cet avion porta SEAC raies
d'identité blanches comme illustrées, avec les lettres de série répétées sur
la raie de dérive.

Dessous: Vue agréable en plein vol d'un Catalina IVB construit de
Boeing de numéro de série JX431 et portant la lettre en chiffre
individuelle 'A' sur la dérive.

Pages 28–29: Republic Thunderbolt Mk I, FL792, de No. 268 Sqn.,
Yelahanka, 1944. Fini en camouflage brun foncé/vert foncé avec côtés de
dessous grises claires, l'avion tient les carreaux sur le nez adoptés par No.
258 pour l'objet d'identification. Lettres en chiffre sur fuselage furent
18in en hauteur avec toutes rondelles de 16in diamètre.

Page 30 dessus: Consolidated Liberator B. Mk IV, EW287, de No. 355
Sqn., Salbani, fin de 1944–45. Illustré en les nuances olive grise neutre
retenues par la plupart de RAF Liberators en SEAC, cet appareil porte
marquage d'identité d'escadrille sur ses gouvernails de direction, une
habitude adoptée par au moins de quatre Liberator fractions en le région.
L'emblème fut montre seulement sur le côté baborde.

Dessous: Les contours réflèchis d'un Spitfire XIV à Donmuang,
Thailand, après la fin de la guerre.

Page 31 dessus: (A) Insignes d'une palme, No. 135 Sqn. (B) Insignes
d'As de Pique, No. 81 Sqn. (C) Marquage sur empennage, No. 356 Sqn.
Liberator (D) Marquage sur empennage, No. 215 Sqn. Liberator (E)
Marquage sur empennage, No. 99 Sqn. Liberator. (F) Marquage de nez,
Thunderbolt de No. 134 Sqn. (G) Insignes de No. 17 Sqn., Spitfire XIV
(H) Insignes d'un poing à mailles de No. 132 Sqn., Spitfire XIV (I)
Marquage de nez de Liberator B. Mk VI KH108 cru d'avoir été partie de
No. 355 Sqn.

Dessous: Willys Jeep utilisé par No. 17 Sqn., Burma 1942. Il fut
trouvé avec autres véhicules americains, dans un garage birman, et peindu
convenablement pour utilisation par l'escadrille.

Page 32 (1) *Squadron Leader*, Hurricane pilote, 1944. Il porte chemise et
pantalon verts de jungle d'étoffe cellulaire de distribution d'armée,
casque d'aviateur *Type C* de distribution standard avec masque à
oxygène/microphone; et ceinture à sangles de distribution d'armée avec
étui de revolver et cartouchière; écussons de grade passés sur pattes
d'épaule de chemise—un petit chevron entre deux gros chevrons, bleu
clair sur bleu foncé.

(2) RAF personnel rampant, 1944. La première partie de la Far East
guerre fut caractérisée par l'utilisation de vêtements d'exercice de kaki et
casque. En 1943–45 vêtements verts de jungle de cellulaire de coupe
similaire furent distribué et le chapeau à brousse de mode australienne de

feutre kaki fut porté, souvent avec un RAF écusson sur puggri en bleu foncé, bleu clair et rouge foncé. Bottes à jongle légères sont portées de cuir brun avec un fini de suède.

(3) *Deputy Provost Marshal*, 1945. La chemise et le pantalon verts de jongle sont portés avec le RAF calot bleu-gris. Le dernier porte l'écusson d'un albatros couronné avec dorure sur la côté gauche, bien en avant, et deux boutons dorés sur le devant du bord rabattu. Pattes de grade sont passées sur les pattes d'épaule de chemise—ici, celles d'un *Flight Lieutenant*, deux chevrons égals—et le broussard de feutre de ce grade est porté sur le bras droit.

Farbtafeln

Seite 25 oben: Bristol Blenheim Mk I, L1134, No. 62 Sqn., Alor Star, Kadah Province, Dezember 1941. Illustriert in der Oberflächengüte getragen zu der Zeit des 1941 Gefechts hat das flugzeug dunkelbraune/dunkelgrüne Tarnung mit schwarzen Unterseiten.

Unten: Bodenpersonal pausiert fur die Apparat während Wartung eines No. 28 Sqn. Hurricane Mk IIc in Birma.

Seite 26 oben: Westland Lysander, T1688, No. 357 Sqn. in Drigh Road, Juli 1 1945. Dies einzelnes Flugzeug wurde von Fliegeroffizier H. V. D. Hallet gefahren und das Verband wurde gemacht, um Force No. 136 zu hilfen; Farbeneinzelheiten schliessen grune/graue Tarnung, schwarze Unterseiten und gelbes Spinner ein.

Unten: Hawker Hurricane Mk IIb, BE171, No. 17 Sqn. Mingladon, 1942. Ein der ersten Hurricanes in Birma wird dies Luftfahrzeug in *Scheme A* Tarnung mit *Sky Type S* Unterseiten Illustriert; runde Scheiben auf Rumpf 35in Durchmesser und 45in *Type A* auf oberen Tragflächen; 27 × 24 Abzeichen auf der Kielflosse, 8in Serien und 2ft hohe Schlüsselbuchstaben.

Seite 27 oben; Bristol Beaufighter TF Mk X, RD515, No. 22 Sqn., 1945. Mit einer Oberflächengüte meeresgrauer/dunkelgrüner Tarnung mit Mittelmeergrau auf den Unterseiten trug dies Luftfahrzeug weisse SEAC-Identitätstreifen, wie man illustriert hat, mit den Serienbuchstaben auf dem Kielflossestreifen nochmal gezeigt.

Unten: Angenehme Flugaussicht eines Boeing-gebauten Catalina IVB mit der Seriennummer JX431 und tragend den individuellen Schlüsselbuchstaben 'A' auf der Kielflosse.

Seiten 28–29: Republic Thunderbolt Mk I, FL792, No. 268 Sqn., Yelahanka, 1944. Mit einer Oberflächengüte in dunkelbrauner/dunkelgrüner Tarnung mit hellgrauen Unterseiten hat das Luftfahrzeug das Schachmuster auf der Flugzeugstirn adoptiert von

No. 258 fur Identitätabsichten. Rumpfschlüsselnummern waren 18in hoch mit allen runden Scheiben 16in Durchmesser.

Seite 30 oben: Consolidated Liberator B. Mk IV, EW287, No. 355 Sqn., Salbani, spat 1944–45. Illustriert in den amerikanischen oliven graubraunen und farblosgrauen Farbtönen behalten von meisten RAF Liberators in SEAC trägt dies Luftfahrzeug Staffelidenti-tätabzeichen auf seinen Leitwerken, eine Verfahrungsweise am wenigsten von vier Liberator-verbänden in dem Gebiet mitgemacht. Das Abzeichen wurde nur auf der Backbordseite gezeigt.

Unten: Die entschlossene Aussenlinien eines Spitfire XIV in Donmuang, Thailand, nach dem Ende des Kriegs.

Seite 31 oben: (A) Abzeichen einer Palme, No. 135 Sqn. (B) Abzeichen eines Pikas, No. 81 Sqn. (C) Rumpfendeabzeichen, No. 356 Sqn. Liberator. (D) Rumpfendeabzeichen, No. 215 Sqn. Liberator. (E) Rumpfendeabzeichen, No. 99 Sqn. Liberator. (F) Rumpfspiteabzeichen, Thunderbolt No. 134 Sqn. (G) Abzeichen No. 17 Sqn. Spitfire XIV. (H) Abzeichen eines gepanzerten Faust No. 132 Sqn. Spitfire XIV. (I) Rumpfspiteabzeichen Liberator B. Mk VI KH108, das man eines No. 355 Sqn. geglaubt hat.

Unten: Willys Jeep verwendet von No. 17 Sqn., Burma 1942. Es wurde zusammen mit anderen amerikanischen Fahrzeugen in einer birmanischen Garage gefunden und es wurde für Staffelverwendung passend angestrict.

Seite 32: (1) *Squadron Leader*, Hurricane Pilot, 1944. Er trägt ein dschungelgrünes Netzhemd und Hose von der Armee ausgegeben, normalen ausgegebenen *Type C* Fliegerhelm mit Sauerstoffmaske/Mikrophon; und Gurt ausgegeben von der Armee mit Pistolenhalfter und Patronentasche; Dienstgradabzeichen den Achselstücke Hemds übergezogen—ein kleines zwischen zwei grossen Streifen, hellblau auf dunkelblau.

(2) RAF Bodenpersonal, 1944. Der erste Teil des Far East-Kriegs wurde von der Verwendung Drillichs aus Kaki und Helm bezeichnet. In 1943 wurden dschungelgrüne Netzkleidung des gleichen Schnitts und der Hut aus graugelbem Filz in der Mode des australischen Busches oft mit einem RAF-Abzeichen auf dem Puggri in dunkelblau hellblau und dunkelrot ausgegeben. Dünne Dschungelstiefeln aus braunem Leder mit einer Appretur aus Wildleder werden getragen.

(3) *Deputy Provost Marshal*, 1945. Das dschungelgrüne Hemd und die Hose werden mit der RAF blaugrauen Feldmütze getragen. Die Letzte trägt ein Abzeichen eines vergoldeten Albatross auf der linken Seite ganz vorner und zwei goldene Knöpfe auf dem Einsatz der Krempe. Dienstgradabzeichen werden den Achselstücken Hemds übergezogen—hier die eines *Flight Lieutenant*, zwei gleiche Abzeichen—und die Broussard aus Filz dieses Dienstgrads wird auf dem rechten Ärmel getragen.
